THE HARVARD LAMPOON

nightlight

The first volume of the *Harvard Lampoon* appeared in February, 1876. Written by seven undergraduates and modeled on *Punch*, the British humor magazine, the debut issue took the Harvard campus by storm. U.S. President Ulysses S. Grant was advised not to read the magazine, as he would be too much "in stitches" to run the government.

nightlight

a parody

THE HARVARD LAMPOON

Vintage Books

A Division of Random House, Inc.

New York

A VINTAGE ORIGINAL, NOVEMBER 2009

Copyright © 2009 by The Harvard Lampoon, Inc.

All rights reserved. Published in the United States by Vintage Books,
a division of Random House, Inc., New York, and in Canada
by Random House of Canada Limited, Toronto.

Vintage and colophon are registered trademarks of Random House, Inc.

Library of Congress Cataloging-in-Publication Data is available.

ISBN : 978-0-307-47610-4

Book design by Claudia Martinez

www.vintagebooks.com

Printed in the United States of America
10 9 8 7 6 5 4 3 2 1

CONTENTS

🦇 v 🦇

nightlight

1. FIRST LOOK

THE HOT PHOENIX SUN GLARED DOWN ON THE CAR windowsill where my bare, pallid arm dangled shamelessly. My mom and I were both going to the airport, but only I had a ticket waiting for me, and that ticket was one-way.

I had a dejected, brooding expression on my face, and I could tell from the reflection in the window that it was also an intriguing expression. It seemed out of place, coming from a girl in a sleeveless, lacy top and bell-bottom jeans (stars on the back pockets). But I was that kind of girl—out of place. Then I shifted from that place on the dashboard to a normal position in the seat. Much better.

I was exiling myself from my mom's home in Phoenix to my dad's home in Switchblade. As a self-exiled exile, I would know the pain of Diaspora and the pleasure of imposing it, callously disregarding my own pleas to say one last good-bye to the potted fungus I was cultivating. I had to coarsen my skin if I was going to be a refugee in Switchblade, a town in northwest Oregon that no one knows about. Don't try to look it up on a map—it's not *important* enough for *mapmakers* to care about. And don't even think about looking me up on that map—apparently, I'm not important enough either.

"Belle," my mom pouted in the terminal. I felt a pang of guilt, leaving her to fend for herself in this huge, friendless airport. But, as the pediatrician said, I couldn't let her separation anxiety prevent me from getting out of the house for eight or so years.

I got down on my knees and held her hands. "Belle is only going to be gone for *the rest of high school*, okay? You're going to have a lot of fun with Bill, right Bill?"

Bill nodded. He was my new stepdad and the only other person available to take care of her while I was gone. I can't say I trusted him, but he was cheaper than a sitter.

I straightened up and crossed my arms. It was time to cut the crap. "The emergency numbers are above the phone in the kitchen," I told him. "If she gets hurt, skip the first two—they're your cell phone and Domino's. I've cooked enough meals to last you both the first month if you split one-third of a Stouffer's Lasagna a day."

My mom smiled at the thought of lasagna.

"You don't have to go, Belle," said Bill. "Sure, my street-hockey team is going on tour, but only around the neighborhood. There's plenty of space in the car for you, your mom and me to live."

"It's no big deal. I want to go. I want to leave all of my friends and the sunlight for a small, rainy town. Making you happy makes me happy."

"Please stay—who will pay the bills when you leave?"

I could hear my boarding number being called. "I bet Bill can run faster than Mom to the nice Jamba Juice man!"

"I am the fastest!" my mom shouted. As they ran off, Bill pulling her shirt to get ahead, I slowly backed away into the gate, through the jet bridge, and onto the plane. None of us were very good at saying good-bye. For some reason, it always came out good-BUH.

I was nervous about reuniting with my dad. He could be distant. Twenty-seven years of being the only window-wiper in Switchblade had forced him to distance himself from others by at least a windowpane. I recall my mom breaking down crying on the sofa after one of their rows and him just watching her stoically, right outside the window, wiping in powerful, circular motions.

When I saw him waiting for me outside the terminal, I walked towards him shyly, tripping over a toddler and soaring into a keychain display. Embarrassed, I straightened up and fell down the escalator, somersaulting over the roller luggage inconsiderately placed on the left side. I get my lack of coordination from my dad, who always used to push me down when I was learning how to walk.

"Are you all right?" my dad laughed, steadying me as I

got off. "That's my clumsy old Belle!" he added, pointing to another girl.

"It's me! I'm your Belle," I cried, covering my face with my hair like I normally wear it.

"Oh! Hello! It's good to see you, Belle." He gave me a firm, gripping hug.

"It's good to see you, too, *Dad*." How strange it felt to use that moniker. At home in Phoenix, I called him Jim and my mom called him Dad.

"You've grown so big—I didn't recognize you without the umbilical cord, I suppose."

Had it really been that long? Had I really not seen my dad since I was thirteen and going through my pet umbilical cord phase? I realized we had a lot of catching up to do.

I hadn't brought all of my clothes from Phoenix, so I only had twelve bags. My dad and I took them in shifts to his Viper.

"Before you start making jabs about me being divorced, middle-aged, and going through a midlife crisis," he said as we put on our seat belts, ankle straps, and helmets, "allow me to explain that I *need* a very aerodynamic car as a window-wiper. My customers are judgmental people—if I don't drag race to those windows, they're going to question whether I'm the right kind of guy to hang off of their roofs. Push that button, hon—it raises the giant snake head."

I hoped he wasn't thinking of driving me to school in that car. Every other kid probably rode a donkey.

"I got you your own car," my dad said, after I counted

down and said "blast off!" He started the car after turning the key in the ignition several times.

"What kind of car?" My Dad really loved me, so I was pretty sure it was an airplane-car.

"A truck car. A U-HAUL, to be exact. I got it pretty cheap. Free, to be exact."

"Where did you get it from?" I asked, hoping he wouldn't say the dump.

"The street."

Phew. "Who sold it to you?"

"Don't worry about it. It's a gift."

I couldn't believe it. A huge truck to store all of the bottle caps I've always wanted to start collecting.

I turned my attention to the window, which was reflecting a flushed, pleased expression. Beyond that the rain poured hard on the green town of Switchblade. The too green town. In Phoenix, the only green things are traffic lights and alien flesh. Here, nature was green.

The house was a two-story Tudor, cream with chocolate timbering, like a miniature éclair that makes you fat for days. It was almost completely blocked from view by my truck, which had a large graphic on the side of a lumberjack sawing a tree, with "U-HAUL" written above.

"The truck is beautiful." I breathed. I exhaled. Then I breathed again. "Beautiful."

"I'm glad you like it, because it's all yours."

I looked at my huge, unwieldy truck and pictured it in the school parking lot surrounded by flashy sports cars. Then

I pictured it eating those other cars. I could not stop smiling.

I knew my dad would insist on carrying my twelve bags into the house all by himself, so I ran ahead to my room. It looked familiar. Four walls and a ceiling, just like my old room in Phoenix! Leave it to my dad to find little ways to make me feel at home.

One nice thing about my dad is, as an old person, his hearing isn't too great. So when I closed the door to my room, unpacked, cried uncontrollably, slammed the door, and threw my clothes around my room in a fit of dejected rage, he didn't notice. It was a relief to let some of my steam out, but I wasn't ready to let all of it out yet. That would come later, when my dad was asleep and I was lying awake thinking about how ordinary kids my age are. If only one of them were extraordinary, then I'd be rid of this insomnia.

I picked at my breakfast the next morning. The only cereal dad had in his cupboard was fish flakes. After getting dressed, I looked in the mirror. Staring back was a sallow-cheeked girl with long, dark hair, pale skin and dark eyes. Just kidding! That would be so scary. Staring back was me. I quickly combed my hair and picked up my backpack, sighing as I shimmied up the rope into my U-HAUL. I hoped there wouldn't be any vampires at this school.

In the school parking lot, I parked my truck in the only place it would fit: the principal's space and the vice principal's space. Besides my truck, the only other car that stood out was a racecar with antennas stuck all over the top. *What kind of a human would drive such a posh vehicle?* I wondered as I walked through the heavy front doors. Not any kind of human I'd ever met.

A red-haired woman sat at the desk in the administration office. "What can I do for you?" she asked, eyeing me through her spectacles, trying to judge me by my looks. As a deeply mysterious person, however, I defy such judgments. She was pale, like me, but in a large, obese way.

"You don't recognize me—I'm new here," I said strategically. The last thing the mayor needed right now was for the window-wiper's daughter to be kidnapped. But sure enough, she kept looking at me. My fame had preceded me.

"And what can I do for you?" she repeated.

I knew that she probably only wanted to help me because I was the window-wiper's daughter, the girl everyone had been talking about since my plane got in yesterday. And I knew what they must say about me: "Belle Goose: queen, warrior, chapter-book reader." I cleverly decided to play into their preconception.

"Salut! Comment allez-vous s'il vous plait . . . Oh, I'm sorry. How embarrassing. I took French at my old high school in Phoenix—sometimes I just slip into it. Anyway, to put it in English, can you direct me to my next class?"

"Sure. Let's take a look at your schedule . . ."

I pulled it from my bag and released it into her pallid, chubby fingers, one of which was squeezed through a diamond ring like a sausage through a slipknot. I smiled at her. She looked like she would make a grateful wife.

"It looks like your first class is English."

"But I've already taken English. A few semesters of it, actually."

"Don't be smart with me, young lady."

So, she knew I was smart. Flattered, I conceded.

"You know what?" I said. "I'll go. What the heck, right?"

"Down the hall to your right," she told me. "Room 201."

"Thank you," I said. It wasn't even noon yet, and I'd already made a friend. Was I some kind of people-magnet? Granted, she was a middle-aged woman, but that made sense. My mom always told me I was mature for my age, especially because I *enjoy* the taste of coffee with hot chocolate and sugar and milk. I sauntered maturely over to Room 201, flung open the door and peered at the students with my chin out. The whole class could tell I was friends with older people.

The teacher scanned his attendance list. "And you must be . . . Belle Goose."

All of this attention was getting a little embarrassing.

"Take a seat," he said.

Unfortunately, the class was too basic to hold my interest: *Ulysses*, *Gravity's Rainbow*, *Oblivion*, and *Atlas Shrugged*, supplemented with the various lenses of Derrida, Foucault, Freud, Dr. Phil, Dr. Dre, and Dr. Seuss. I groaned loudly as the teacher droned on, introducing everyone's name. I'd have to ask my mom to send me some interesting literature, like those essays I wrote last year.

When the bell rang, the boy next to me predictably turned to me and started talking.

"Excuse me," he said, hoping I would fall in love with him or something. "Your bag is in my way."

I knew it. He was totally the "your-bag-is-in-my-way" type.

"My name is Belle," I said. I wondered which was the more surprising part about me—my elbows, which are naturally pointy, or my demeanor, which is apathetic to popularity, even though I've read all the popularity handbooks so I could be popular if I tried." You can walk me to my next class."

"Um, sure," he said, wanting me. He made small talk on the way about how he was abandoned as a child and will only rest easy once he is avenged. His name was Tom. I could tell people passing by were listening in, hoping that I would reveal the mystery of my past.

"So what's Phoenix like?" he beseeched.

"It's hot there. And sunny all the time."

"Really? Wow."

"You sound surprised. You must be surprised by how fair-skinned I am, coming from such a hot climate."

"Hmm. I suppose you are pale."

"Yeah—I'm half dead," I joked, very humorously. He didn't laugh. I should have known no one would get my sense of humor in Switchblade. It was like no one here had ever told a sarcasm before.

"Here's your class," he said when we reached the Trigonometry classroom. "Good luck!"

"Thanks. Maybe we'll have another class together," I said, giving him something to live for.

Trigonometry was all blah-blah formulas that we'd just save on our calculators anyway and Government was all blah-blah tomorrow we're crossing the border to attack Canada. Nothing I hadn't done at my old school.

One girl walked with me to the cafeteria for lunch. She had brown bushy hair in a ponytail that was more like a squirrel tail in the context of her beady squirrel eyes. I thought I recognized her from somewhere, but I couldn't place it.

"Hi," she said. "I think I'm in all your classes." So *that's* why I recognized her. She reminded me of a squirrel I hung out with in Phoenix.

"I'm Belle."

"I know. We've introduced ourselves already. Like, four times."

"Oh, sorry. I have a hard time remembering things that won't be useful to me later."

She told me her name again. Lululu? Zagraziea? It was one of those forgettable names. She asked if I wanted to eat with her. I stopped in the hallway, opened up my date book, and looked at Monday, 12:00.

"Blank!" I exclaimed. I penciled in "Lunch with classmate" then checked it off while we stood in line. This was the year I would become organized.

We sat at a table with Tom and some other ordinaries. They kept asking me probing questions about what my interests were. I gently explained that that was between me and my potential friends.

It was then that I saw him. He was sitting at a table all by himself, not even eating. He had an entire tray of baked potatoes in front of him and still he did not touch a single one. How could a human have his pick of baked potatoes and resist them all? Even odder, he hadn't noticed me, Belle Goose, future Academy Award winner.

A computer sat before him on the table. He stared intently at the screen, narrowing his eyes into slits and concentrating those slits on the screen as if the only thing that mattered to him was physically dominating that screen. He was muscular, like a man who could pin you up against the wall as easily as a poster, yet lean, like a man who would rather cradle you in his arms. He had reddish, blonde-brown hair that was groomed heterosexually. He looked older than the other boys in the room—maybe not as old as God or my father, but certainly a viable replacement. Imagine if you took every woman's idea of a hot guy and averaged it out into one man. This was that man.

"What is that?" I asked, knowing that whatever it was it wasn't avian.

"That's Edwart Mullen," Lululu said.

Edwart. I had never met a boy named Edwart before. Actually, I had never met any human named Edwart before. It was a funny sounding name. *Much* funnier than Edward.

As we sat there, gazing at him for what seemed like

hours but couldn't have been more than the entire lunch period, his eyes suddenly flicked towards me, slithering over my face and boring into my heart like fangs. Then in a flash they went back to glowering at that screen.

"He moved here two years ago from Alaska," she said.

So not only was he pale like me, but he was also an outsider from a state that begins with an "A." I felt a surge of empathy. I had never felt a connection like this before.

"That boy's not worth your time," she said, wrongly. "Edwart doesn't date."

I smirked inwardly and snorted outwardly, tucking the soda-mucous that flew out into my pocket. So, I would be his first girlfriend.

She got up to leave. "Coming to Bio, Belle?"

"Duh, Lululu," I said.

"Lucy. My name is Lucy— As in *I Love Lucy*."

"All right. Lucy— As in *I Love Edwart*." Maybe I'm special, but I've always had a knack for remembering mnemonics. "Trash to the left," I bellowed, throwing out my leftovers—a *half*-eaten cake. I looked back at Edwart to see if he had noticed that I, too, am a disciplined eater. But strangely, he was gone. In the ten minutes since I had last looked at him, he had vanished into thin air.

I turned around just in time to see that I'd missed the trashcan by a lot, and my *half*-eaten cake was flying towardss the back of a girl sitting at a nearby table.

"HEY!" she said, as the cake made impact. "Who did that?"

"Let's go," I said to Lucy, grabbing her arm and running out of the cafeteria as the food fight began.

When Lucy and I got to class she went to sit with her lab partner and I looked around for an empty seat. There were two left: one near the front of the room and one next to Edwart. Since the front chair had a wobbly leg after I walked past and kicked it in, there was no choice. I had to sit next to the hottest boy in the room.

I walked towards the seat, circling my hips and raising my eyebrows rhythmically like an attractive person. Suddenly I was falling forwards, sliding down the aisle from the momentous force of my plunge. Luckily, a computer wire wrapped around my ankle and stopped me from slamming into Mr. Franklin's desk. I quickly pulled it from the wall to untangle myself, stood up, and looked around casually to see if anyone had seen. The whole class was looking at me, but probably for a different reason—I had a hologram patch on my backpack. From one angle it was an eggplant, from another it was an aubergine.

Edwart was looking at me, too. Maybe it was the fluorescent lighting, but his eyes seemed darker—soulless. He was seething furiously. His computer was open in front of him, and the synthesized melody from before had ceased. He raised his fist at me in anger.

I wiped the chemical dust off my clothes and sat down. Without looking at Edwart, I pulled out my textbook and notepad. Then, without looking at Edwart, I looked at the board and wrote down the terms Mr. Franklin had written. I don't think other people in my situation could do quite so many things without looking at Edwart.

Facing straight ahead, I let my eyes sort of slide to the side and study him peripherally, which doesn't count as looking. He had moved his computer to his lap and resumed playing his game. We were sitting side by side at the lab counter, yet he hadn't started a conversation with me. It was as though I hadn't applied deodorant or something when in reality I had applied deodorant, perfume, and Febreze. Was my lip gloss smudged or something? I took out my compact mirror to check. Nope, but I did have a few developing pimples up by the hairline. I picked up a pencil on Edwart's desk and pressed it against the soft, supple flesh of my face. They were the projectile kind. Satisfaction attained.

I turned to thank him kindly for the use of his pencil, but he was looking at me in horror, his mouth agape, an open invitation to all sorts of airborne organisms like birds. He grabbed the pencil and started wiping his hands with baby-wipes and rubbing the pencil with Purell. Then he drew a circle around himself in chalk and returned to copying notes from the board, singing this jingle amiably to himself:

"Germs contagious. Contagion alert. But Edwart and Purell are stronger than dirt."

I reached out to borrow the pencil again for my notes, but the moment my hand breached the chalk line he screamed. It was an unnaturally high pitch for a boy. The right pitch for a superhero, though.

Mr. Franklin was talking about flow cytometry, immunorecipitation and DNA microarrays, but I already knew that stuff from the audiotape I listened to in my truck that morning on my way to school. I moved my eyes in circles, like they were on a Ferris wheel. This is the best way I know of to keep myself from falling asleep. Every time my eyes moved towards the right, though, they kind of hovered there for a little bit. I couldn't help it—they wanted to see Edwart. Then my eyes would go to the top of the sockets towards the ceiling and stop because, hey, nice view.

Edwart continued to jab at his computer. With each pounding finger I could see the blood surging through the bulging veins on his forearms to his biceps, straining against the tight-fitted, white Oxford shirt pushed cavalierly to his elbows as though he had a lot of manual labor to do. Why was he typing so loudly? Was he trying to tell me something? Was he trying to prove how easy it would be for him to fling me up into the sky and then catch me tightly in his arms, whispering that he would never share me with anyone else in the entire world? I shuddered and smiled coyly, terrified.

When the bell rang I stole another glance at him and shrank into a deeper sense of worthlessness. He was now staring furiously up at the bell, shaking all the muscles in his fist at it, glowering at it with his dark, heated eyes and loathing lashes. He clenched his hair in exasperation, clinging to the tussled tufts as he raised his head to the ceiling. Then he slowly turned to me. Looking into his eyes I felt waves of electricity, currents of electrons charging towards me. Was this how it felt to be in love, I wondered, for robots? Caught in his ionized hypnosis, the old adage came to mind: *Beautiful enough to kill, gut, stuff, and frame above your fireplace.*

Suddenly, he jerked out of his daze and sprinted for the door. As he ran, I noticed how tall he was, his long legs leaping in strides the size of my entire body, his arms so firm the impact didn't make a ripple. My eyes welled. I hadn't seen something this beautiful since I was a kid and the Skittles in my sweaty fist turned my hand rainbow. His shoulder blades jutted against his shirt as he ran. They looked like white wings beating majestically before takeoff. Demonic white wings.

"Wait!" I called after him. He had left his computer at his seat. "Game Over," the screen read. Game over, indeed, I thought, using a metaphor.

"Can I copy your notes?" asked a regular human male. I looked up and saw a boy of medium height, with dark hair and a lean but muscular frame. I felt drawn to him. He smiled at me. I lost interest.

"Sure, whatever," I said, handing him my notepad and suddenly noticing that I had doodled a picture of Edwart. In the drawing he had fangs, dripping with a dark substance. Soy sauce.

"I'm going to need that back," I said. That drawing was going on my wall.

"Thanks, Lindsey," he said, mistaking me for Lindsey Lohan. He smiled again. What a nice boy. He had nice neat hair and nice clear eyes. We were going to be great friends. Great Just Friends.

"Walk me to the administration office," I said. We all had gym next, but I needed my wheelchair. I have a condition which makes my legs become paralyzed every time I think about gyms.

"Okay," he said, letting me put my weight on him. "I'm Adam, by the way. I think I saw you in my English class. That'll be great! As long as one of us takes notes, the other one—me—doesn't have to go to class." He was getting kind of out of breath as he dragged me along. Being close to me makes some guys nervous.

"Did you notice anything funny about Edwart in class? I think I love him," I said nonchalantly.

"Well, he did look kind of angry when you fell and disconnected his computer charger."

So it wasn't all in my mind; others had noticed Edwart's awareness of me. There was something about me that evoked very strong feelings in Edwart.

"Hmm," I said scientifically. "How interesting."

"Here we are." After propping me upright against the wall, Adam staggered backwards, huffing and puffing.

I dismissed him and stepped inside the office.

"I'm paralyzed for the next hour," I announced to the secretary.

"Go sit in your car, dear," she said, looking up from her copy of *Daylight*.

I skipped outside to my car, trying to daydream about

its powers as king of the cars, but I was too disturbed. First of all, if I had gotten my car for free, that meant that everyone else had paid *more* money for *tinier* cars. Secondly, I was pretty sure there was something supernatural about Edwart—something beyond rational speculation.

So I stopped speculating about him and watched a procession of ants go by. Life would be much easier if I could carry things twenty times my body weight.

2. RESCUE

THE NEXT DAY WAS WONDERFUL . . . AND TERRIBLE.
So, overall, I guess it was okay.

It was wonderful because it was raining less. It was
terrible because Tom hit me with his car.

"I'm so sorry— I didn't see you!" he said, driving away
to find a parking space before the lot filled up. I picked
myself up and smiled knowingly. Tom's constant attempts to
get my attention were flattering and sometimes surprising.

Adam sat next to me in English again. I began to worry
that this would become a pattern, that he would expect to
occupy the seat next to me *forever*, even when I was just eating breakfast at home with my Dad. Mr. Schwartz called on
him and he mumbled something—I think that the sombrero
I was wearing was both alluring and practical for the
weather—but my mind had drifted. I was thinking about

Edwart. I took out the list I made of rational reasons he wouldn't talk to me:

> —too scared
> —too sad
> —too mute
> —not human

I was about to start a new list, Places I'd Like to Visit, when I heard someone saying my name.

I looked up. It was Adam.

"Class is over," he said, and walked out. I wasn't used to all this attention from boys.

"Yeah," I called after him. "I knew the whole time!" He didn't respond. I sighed. I should have known no one would get my sense of humor in English class.

On my way out, I bumped into a desk, which bumped into another desk, which bumped into a table with a Popsicle-stick and marshmallow model of the Globe Theatre on top of it. The model wobbled dangerously. Knowing my luck, it is a miracle it didn't topple over onto the desk. Instead, it toppled onto the floor, where I accidentally slipped on it and somehow got marshmallow in my hair.

At lunch I sat with Tom and Lucy's friends again. Looking around at all the other tables, I realized this must be the popular table. It was definitely the closest to the door—optimal for getting to class on time. Also, everyone at the table had a bag lunch with their name on it. I felt bad for the kids at other tables, who were probably nice, but just not socially connected enough to sit close to the door or use paper bags. Tom's lunch had "My Little Sugar-Pie" written on it. When I asked him why his mom only made him a little sugar-pie, he pretended not to hear. I made a note to pack some vegetables for that boy.

After lunch was Biology—with Edwart. I wished my heart wasn't beating so fast as I walked down the hall. I especially wished my armpits weren't sweating so much; I must be secreting pheromones like crazy, which would only heighten Adam and Tom's frenzy. Drenched in my natural secretions, I walked into class and braced myself for their wild attacks. Instead, I saw Edwart. He looked like a boy in an ad for deodorant, which I definitely would have bought if he were selling it, even if it had aluminum in it, which causes AIDS. I slid into the seat next to him. To my astonishment, he looked up from his computer with a slight nod.

"Hi," he said in the quiet voice of a boys' choir of angels.

I couldn't believe he was talking to me. He was sitting as far away from me as last time, probably because of the smell, but he seemed to know I was there instinctively, like some sort of animal.

"Hi," I said. "How did you know my name was Belle?"

"What? Oh, I didn't know that. Hi, Belle."

"Yeah, Belle. How did you know that? Belle is a nickname."

He looked about confusedly. "I'm sorry. I—"

"Don't worry about it," I said, looking towards the

blackboard. "I'm sure there's a *perfectly rational* explanation for all of this." After that he stopped talking. I doodled a picture of what I'd look like if I got bitten by a vampire. I'd look very feminine.

Mr. Franklin explained that we were going to dissect a frog in class today. He gave each group a specimen, taken from a cold, anesthetic-smelling plastic bag. Our frog lay in the metal tray on our table, lifeless. It made me shudder to think of all the harmless flies it had probably eaten.

"So . . . should we start?" Edwart asked.

"Yeah, yeah," I said quickly. I picked up the knife, and stuck it into our frog.

"Wait!" Edwart declared. "You have to read the procedure first!"

"It's so easy," I said, slicing the frog down its middle. I'd done this lab before. At a pond, when I was a little girl.

Mr. Franklin came over to our table. "Careful there, Belle! You want to be able to examine the inside!"

"I know," I acknowledged. "I *was* in the advanced class at my old school."

Mr. Franklin nodded, "I see," he postulated. "Why don't you let Edwart handle the rest of this dissection?"

I shrugged. It didn't matter to me; if Mr. Franklin thought this lab was too easy for me, he was right. I leaned back in my chair, bored already. Edwart carefully stripped away layers of the frog's skin and made notes on his diagram. I leaned forwards, suddenly mesmerized by his handwriting. For a second I thought that maybe I was looking at the handwriting of an angel. Then I remembered angels don't have hands. He must be something else—something else *supernatural*.

"So . . . uh . . . are you going to write any of this down in your lab report?" Edwart asked. He held up his sheet for me to copy, as if just because he did all the observing, he knew more about frog organs than I did.

"I already finished it," I told him. I held up my sheet. I had drawn much more advanced pictures depicting what it would look like if you removed a human's organs and replaced them with those of a frog. Below the diagrams, I listed a few organizations that take organ donations in case Mr. Franklin wanted to do the charitable thing and donate all these frog organs to people who needed them.

Edwart looked at my picture and frowned, suddenly ashamed of his own report in comparison. "Let's turn our labs in individually," he said, knowing I deserved all the credit. As he spoke, his eyes lit up a brilliant green.

"Were your eyes green yesterday?" I asked quickly.

He looked at me with a blank stare—the blank stare of a god. The kind of god in a commercial for a hubcap repair shop.

"Well, yeah. I mean, I have green eyes," he said.

The bell rang, and I started in my seat. I had lost track of time, staring into Edwart's odd green eyes. He hurriedly left the classroom. I exhaled and inhaled deeply, trying to breathe in his scent, but all I could smell was lab frog. I stood up, knocking over several other students.

• • •

I checked my e-mail after school, and I already had forty-four e-mails from my mom. I clicked one at random.

> Belle! Answer this e-mail right now or I'm calling the police! Too late! I just called the police! They're asking me if it's an emergency and I'm saying yes! I'm saying you've been ignoring your mother! I'm saying you're being held hostage at a dock! That should do it. Love, Mom

I quickly wrote her back, trying to sound as cheerful as possible, but it was hard to conceal my depression from her. She knew me too well. She knew that when I wrote that I had met a nice girl to be friends with, it meant that most of the people at school were boring. She knew that when I said Dad and I were getting along fine and he had even bought me a car, it meant that a demonic boy at school was being mean to me. Thank God we came up with this secret code when I was little to confuse cyber-stalkers. I wanted to tell her that Switchblade wasn't so bad. If only something dangerous would happen. Or not necessarily some*thing* dangerous, but some*one* dangerous. Then maybe my Mom wouldn't have to be so concerned for my well-being.

I whipped up a few racks of lamb for dinner.

"Belle, you really didn't have—" my dad began as he sat down at the table.

"No, Dad," I said. "I used to cook all the time in Phoenix. Really. It's fine."

"I wish you'd let me cook every once in a while," he said. "It's just—I mean, I love your cooking, but I told you I was a vegetarian, and . . ."

"You don't like it, Dad?" I asked concernedly, worried that I hadn't cut the meat into small enough pieces or fun enough shapes.

"No, no, it's great, Belle. I know it's been hard for you here. It's great."

I smiled as he took another bite. At least Dad was trusting me a little more in the kitchen.

By the next morning, the rain had turned to snow. I wasn't too thrilled. I liked being able to travel to and from class via puddle, jumping from one to the next and rating the puddle on the Belle-Goose scale—a scale from 1-5 where 1 represents dry land and 5 represents a tsunami. Jim had already left by the time I got up. I spent a half-hour worrying that he hadn't found the bread I had left for him in the cabinet, or the milk I had left in the milk-carton. Then I put on my puffiest snow-cape and hurried outside.

My U-HAUL was snowed in, but fortunately I have arms—optimal for picking up huge amounts of snow and putting it elsewhere. The only trouble was, I didn't have any place to put the snow besides my front yard. So, I put the piles in the back of my U-HAUL. Then I realized this was a great opportunity to make a giant slushie. I ran back inside for the sugar and red food coloring. I sprinkled both onto the snow. As I started the truck, I thought about what I'd name my cooking show. The first thing that came to my mind was: *Goose Cooks Geese.* The second thing that came to my mind was: "Perfect!"

I kept hitting the breaks as I drove to avoid skidding on ice and to create a rocking sensation in my U-HAUL that would mix all the ingredients in the back into one delicious slushie. At red lights, I simulated ice-cream truck music by humming.

When it snows, the rules of parking no longer apply, so I stopped in the street and began to walk towards the school's side entrance. That's when it happened.

It wasn't in slow motion, like an old person walking, but it also wasn't in fast motion, like an old person running. It was like when you sip an energy drink with a skull on it, even though your mom said not to, and your brain kind of speeds up as you sip and then goes slower as you swallow and then speeds up and goes slower until you throw up. And then you drink another one on a dare.

It was careening towards me across the sky in a perfect arc, careening so quickly that I knew I wouldn't be able to get out of the way. I'd never imagined how I would die, but I had kind of hoped it would be in a war. I had never thought it would be like this: by snowball.

And then suddenly, Edwart was in front of me, his dark, curly-yet-disheveled tresses blocking my view as I heard a giant *squish.* I couldn't believe it. It wasn't even pos-sible. Edwart had saved me.

"How did you—how?" I asked, looking from my perfectly pristine snow-cape to his jacket, soiled with snow. But Edwart wasn't listening. A wide, almost otherworldly grin was spreading across his face.

"Prepare for doom, Nemesis!" he hollered, gathering up some snow and hurling it towardss the school.

I couldn't believe it. Now Edwart was defending me!

"Edwart! Edwart!" I screamed, relinquishing any attempt at self-control. I rushed towardss him as he swiftly bent down to pick up more snow. Pinning his arms to his back, I stopped him from exciting the snowball-hurler any further. "You saved my life!" I cried. "Isn't that enough? Stop this endless cycle of vengeance!" I perched on his back to stop him from the demonic violence he was capable of, two snowballs hit him in the face.

"Uhh," he said, freeing his arms and brushing the snow from his eyes. "Hey, get off me, you girl! You're going to make me smell like girl things!"

I let go, mesmerized. The snow was dripping off his coat, almost as if *it didn't stick to him*.

"How are you doing that?" I asked, successfully concealing my absolute terror of his superhuman force.

"Edwart has a girlfriend, Edwart has a girlfriend," someone shouted.

"I do not! She is not! I do not know her!" he yelled, protecting our blossoming mutual intrigue from petty rumors before turning back to me. "What?" he asked. "How am I doing what?"

"The snow! It's melting off you!" I took a step closer until our faces were nearly touching. "You're— you're not human, are you?" I whispered intimately.

He laughed a little. Nervously.

"Is this about Biology class?" he asked. "Because I only knew all that stuff about frogs because I once had a frog. It's not like I go on Internet sites to practice dissection or anything like that. Like nerds do. I don't even study for class. Or get good grades. I hate school things. I mean, it's like, why don't we all just skip class and, like, hang. You know?"

I was suddenly blushing. His shoes, covered in dirty snow, were too beautiful to be real. I bent down to investigate, poking them with my finger. He pulled his foot away quickly and nearly fell over. Miraculously, he regained balance by *simply putting his foot down.*

"Hey! Stop!" he cried. "Do you . . . so do you like games and stuff? Like, video games . . . computer games . . . board games . . . potato chips . . ."

His attempts to evade my question only infuriated me more. I stood up. "I know what I saw— someday, you will trust me enough to tell me the truth."

"The truth about what? I'll tell you now— about bull-frogs?" He laughed. "That's easy. The truth is, they absorb air through their skin."

I looked over my shoulder to protect him from any listeners. There were definitely a few perked ears thirty feet away. "The truth about your *abilities*," I said, raising my eyebrows. I meant to raise only one like they do in detective movies but as soon as I raised one the other sidled up as well. All I knew was, no average human would be able to jump from the sidewalk to the gutter as fast as he did.

"Listen," he whispered ferociously, like a ferocious breeze or very gentle hurricane. "I am an average student, like everybody else. I do normal things on the weekend. Everyday after school, I go back to my house and chill and hang until bedtime, which is whenever I want it to be because my parents are too negligent with me to set a curfew. Understand?" He gripped my shoulders tightly. I knew if I didn't concede, he would easily crush me.

"Yes. I understand. But this isn't the last you'll hear from me," I muttered.

That seemed to appease him. He released my shoulders and ran away, flailing his limbs in that graceful way he had.

I fumed all the way to class. How did he know we were in Bio together? How did he know to walk in front of me at the *exact moment* a snowball was coming? Why did the snowballs melt off him as if they were made of some watery substance? Most of all, why was he lying to me about his true superhuman identity? I was so upset, I accidentally started a fire in math, sending one boy to the nurse's office. I guess I had been rubbing the sticks I carry with me together so hard that, whoops, I started kindling a flame. Gee. Edwart was really taking over my brain. I couldn't concentrate on anything, not even taking the Riemann sum of the approximate distances traveled in each integral of the problem I was working on. Boy, was I all out of sorts.

That night I had my first dream about Edwart Mullen. Carnival music was playing, and I was sitting in a colorful tent, surrounded by animals. We were all eating popcorn together and joking around. Suddenly, the tent went dark, and Edwart entered the stage, alone. He was wearing stilts and saying, "Whoa! Whoa!" as he walked in a wobbly way.

I woke up in a cold sweat, terrified.

3. HAND PRICK

THE MONTH FOLLOWING THE SNOWBALL ACCIDENT
was tough. People kept looking at me, especially when teachers
read my name on the attendance list and I said "Here." Somehow my new nickname for Edwart, "Hero," didn't catch on. So,
I decided to break my unwritten, unspoken, and unthought
understanding with Edwart, and start telling our story.

First, I told Tom and Lucy that Edwart saved me from
a snowball. They weren't impressed. So I started saying
Edwart saved me from a rock with snow around it, and, later,
I started saying he saved me from an avalanche. One day, I
said that Edwart ran with superhuman speed, stopping a car
that was about to hit me with his superhuman strength.

"Wait," said the freshman girl in the cafeteria lunch
line. "Edwart Mullen? You mean the kid whose clothes are
too small?"

We looked over at Edwart, who was sitting alone, doing homework due next month.

"Yes," I said gravely, taking a large bite of my pudding to prevent me from saying anything else.

"You must be new here," the girl said, picking up her tray.

"Mumph bleh," I said, spitting little flecks of chocolate pudding after her. She didn't answer. I knew no one would understand me in Switchblade.

Still, Edwart was cold towards me. I knew that he wished it had never happened—that he had never saved me—that I had never started wearing a shirt that said "Thank you, Edwart!" One afternoon in Biology, over a month after the accident, I couldn't take it much longer. Edwart looked so cute with his red curly hair and freckles, like the "before" picture in an ad for freckle concealer for men. Yet he was so complacent, as if he didn't need me and my alluring ear-shape to pass on to his offspring. I had to do something.

I poked the boy in front of me. He turned around, looking surprised.

"Hey, it's Peter, right?" I asked.

"Yeah," he answered, seduced.

"Want to go to prom with me?" I asked, plenty loud so Edwart could hear.

"Um . . . sure," he said. "Would it be okay if we hung out a couple of times before then? I don't really know you."

Did Edwart notice? Was he jealous? I slyly looked at

his mood ring to find out. Still purplish-brown! Clearly, I was going to have to do more—*one* date to prom wasn't enough. I turned to the boy sitting behind me, to the right.

"Zack," I said.

"What is it?" he asked, looking up at the board to take notes.

"Will you go to prom with me?"

"But . . . didn't you just ask Peter?"

"Yeah," I said. "I want to go with you, too."

He hesitated. "Well, I don't have a date yet, so, okay, I guess."

"Hey, Adam," I called across the room.

"Belle, please. I'm trying to teach," said Mr. Franklin. But when I called out to Adam he must have understood that this was an important interruption—an interruption for love—because he just sighed and continued diagramming the cell.

"I already have a date, Belle," Adam whispered loudly.

"Tom!" I shouted.

"Belle!" Mr. Franklin yelled.

I settled down in my chair, satisfied. Edwart was looking now.

The rain was so bad by the time school got out I had to float my U-HAUL back home. I stood on the top of the truck and guided it with a long pole, pretending I was in New Orleans, about to save Edwart from the flood.

"So Belle . . ." my dad said that evening at dinner.

"Any boys at school catch your eye? How about Tom Newt? He seems nice."

"Yeah, I guess," I said, imagining what Tom would look like as Edwart. He would look hot. "Are you going to eat your spinach?"

"Do you want it, honey?"

"No, you should eat it," I said. "And mine, too. It's good for your health. C'mon, dad. Open up!"

I put as much spinach as I could on my fork and moved it towards his mouth. Some spinach fell onto his placemat. Some onto his lap.

"The train's coming! Cug-a-cug-a-cug-a-coo! coo!" I chanted.

"Belle, that's not the noise a train makes," he said. "They go *chug-a-chug-a*—with a 'ch.'"

"Maybe in Switchblade," I said skeptically. This place certainly was backwards.

I wanted to look especially good in Bio the next day, because I was sure that it was the day Edwart would ask if he could be my third date to prom. That night I wrapped my hair in springs from the armchair in our living room to make it curly. I even put in false teeth. On my way to school the next morning, I felt light and bouncy, but that could be because I'd left in some springs.

I went to the Bio classroom fourth period to be sure I was on time for sixth. It was dark and Mr. Franklin was sorting beakers in the closet. He let me eat my lunch there as long as I covered my desk in aluminum foil for cleanliness.

The bell rang. I sat up super straight in my chair and smiled with my big, straight teeth. Students began to come through the door. Tom, Adam, Lucy, followed by more students. No Edwart. I stopped smiling and removed the teeth. Just when I thought Edwart was a normal, jealous boy, he does something unpredictable, like not show up to class with roses.

"Okay, guys," Mr. Lookner began. "My nephew needs a blood transfusion, so I want to know all of your blood types."

He sounded proud of this idea. He put on a pair of rubber gloves, which made an ominous slap as they hit his skin. I cringed. *Slap. Slap. Slap.*

"Okay, I'll stop," he said. "That's just such a cool sound!"

Still no Edwart. Why *this* day to be absent from Bio? He had been in English. I knew this because I delivered a note to him from the "principal's office" when he was in class. It said "Hey QT." I really wished I were principal of this school. I'd give him so much detention. He deserves it, for cutting class instead of asking me out.

Mr. Franklin was detailing the procedure. "I'll be coming around with a medical consent form, so don't start until I get to you. Those of you who aren't AB can sit in the back and chat." A few kids cheered. "But!" he continued. "Not until I know everyone's blood type. Now, I want you to carefully prick your finger with one of these knives from my kitchen . . ."

He grabbed Adam's hand and cut off a bit of his

pointer finger. Blood spurted out and landed on Mr. Franklin's lab coat and the back of a nearby girl's blouse.

As I watched the dripping arc of crimson, I suddenly felt nauseous. Where *was* he? Why wouldn't he come to class on a day when we were doing such a fun lab?

Suddenly, there he was. Edwart. Edwart, standing there with his short buzz cut and masculine jaw, rough with light hair. There was something red stuck in his teeth. With a rush of nausea, I suddenly understood what he was. *Dentist Patient!*

I realized the whole class was silent, staring at me. I guess I must have said that out loud. Oops. Then I thought, no, that can't be right. Edwart has naturally perfect teeth.

I got out of my seat quickly so I might lightly slap Edwart in the face with my hair. I approached the materials table, where he was standing, shoving a pack of Twizzlers into his backpack. I swung my head . . .

. . . And then the next thing I knew I was looking up at Mr. Franklin and Lucy's faces.

"Hey guys," I said.

"Belle, you fell!" Lucy exclaimed jealously.

"No I didn't."

"Yes, Belle, you tripped on the leg of your chair. I think you were unconscious for a couple of seconds," Mr. Franklin explained.

"Nope," I said.

Mr. Franklin stood up and rubbed both his temples like he was drawing circles there. "Dear God," he muttered. "Why today? Edwart!" he called. "Since you've already done this lab with me during your free track, please take Belle to the nurse."

"Sorry I was late, Mr. Franklin, but the Fed Challenge Team needed a replacement and—"

"Just go," Mr. Franklin said. "And Belle, don't mention anything about what we're doing in class today . . ."

I looked right into Mr. Franklin's eyes. He must be some kind of mad scientist! Conducting secret experiments! If things didn't work out with Edwart, I could always be his Igor, digging up bones and teaching them English for chump change.

"Right," I said, winking at Mr. Franklin with one eye, and then the other, to show that I *really* got it.

"I don't need your help walking!" I insisted angrily as I slithered out of the classroom on my belly.

"Edwart, can you carry her?" Mr. Franklin asked.

"You heard her— she wants some bigger guy to do it," he said, crossing his arms and hunching his back so I could climb onto it more easily. He stiffened as I took his hair into my hands like reigns and gave a gentle kick to get him going. Then he fainted.

"Edwart," I said, poking his crumpled form beneath me. "Are you okay? I think I better carry you to the nurse's."

"No! I can do this!" he said, leaping to his feet. He scooped up my entire eight pounds, four ounces—to be honest, I hadn't weighed myself in a few years—and we walked slowly out of the classroom. "Come on Edwart— a half-step at a time," he muttered quietly, not wanting to disturb my faint slumber. "Okay. Now half step at two times."

I rested my head on his firm, sweaty shoulder. I felt something stroking my hair. Then I felt Edwart put some of my hair up to his nose, leaving it draped above his lip. He looked good with a long, full mustache. Suddenly he released my hair. He took some Purell from his pocket and frantically rubbed it on his mouth.

"So, uh, Belle . . . do you have any pets?"

"No," I said sadly, remembering Jared the Iguana. Eventually, I had to return him to where I found him: Mr. Rich's third grade class.

"My mom won't let me have pets," Edwart said. "It's not because she thinks I'm not responsible or anything. She just thinks I'd be too nervous to care for them, and she's probably right. But," he continued. "I found a bat in my attic and I trapped it! Granted, it was a dead bat."

Bats, huh? I thought, repetitively. *Maybe Edwart had rabies!*

We walked in to the nurse's office. The nurse was an older woman who needed glasses but preferred to wear them around her neck with a colorful lanyard. She looked up from her novel, *Full Moon*. "One sec," she said. "I'm almost done with this chapter." Edwart and I waited.

"Okay," she said. "Come on in here and lie down, and I'll get you some ice for your head."

Edwart let me down and the nurse brought me into the adjoining room with two mat-like beds. Edwart watched me leave him sadly, holding his hand out towardss me. When the nurse turned around, he cleverly disguised this gesture by doing the robot.

After the nurse lay me down, he stood there for a while, looking like the star of an infomercial explaining what happened to his little brother when he smoked weed.

"Don't you have somewhere to be?" the nurse asked after a few minutes.

"Yes."

"Wait," she said suddenly. "Are you Edwart Mullen?. I've been calling you down to the nurse's office every day now for a week! You need to get your shots for your trip to Transylvania."

"No! I don't need shots! You have me confused with someone else! You must be thinking of another boy who is much bigger and braver and has a normal name!"

He turned and ran out of the nurse's office. The nurse was about to follow him, but then she sighed and returned to reading.

I strained my neck to see Edwart go around the corner, eventually getting up from my bed to follow him all the way back to class. *Transylvania*, I thought as I walked past the classrooms. Why did that country sound so familiar? Then I thought, *Maybe Edwart is a foreign exchange student!*

I looked in through the window of our classroom door. Edwart took a seat, next to my empty seat. That's when I realized it didn't matter what he was—5'8" or 6'3" like he said on his medical forms—I loved that crazy superhuman.

Back at the nurse's office, I carefully placed Edwart's medical file back in the "Special Attention" cabinet. What was he hiding, besides multiple food allergies? What *was* he? It was time to do some thinking. I sat down on the floor of the nurse's office and assumed a meditation pose, my hands poised upward on my crossed legs. I murmured, "Ommm."

My mind was moving quickly: the red stuff in Edwart's mouth, his being late to class during the blood lab, the bats, Transylvania . . . It didn't make sense. I thought for a while longer. I took an Odwalla bar break. I thought some more.

Then, suddenly, I remembered the accident, and Edwart's snow-proof body, and his eyes that changed from I-don't-remember to green, and I knew. YES! VAMPIRE!

4. RESEARCHES

WHEN I GOT HOME THAT AFTERNOON, I TOLD MY DAD I had a crime to solve so he'd leave me alone. I was glad I'd set up that detective agency last summer called "Belle Goose on the Loose." I made flyers with a drawing of me as Sherlock Holmes and put them up all around Phoenix. Too bad I only ever got one case: the caper of rampant flyer-littering. The culprit is still at large.

After slamming the door to my room to seem like I was hot on someone's trail, I dug through my unpacked stuff until I found the CD of hyena laughter that my mom's new husband gave me on the day I left the two of them alone in Phoenix. At the time, I couldn't help but think he was trying too hard to get my respect. Now, I was glad to have a distraction from thoughts of Edwart. I put the CD in my CD player, put in my headphones, and lay down on my bed, covering my head with pillows. Still, I thought about the vampire I loved, so I put a couple of suitcases on my head.

Once the CD finished, I knew I couldn't stall any longer. It was 1:00 a.m.—the time of night when I research the paranormal. My Internet works via tin-can telephones. One tin can is in the back of our computer, and the other tin can is in the back of our neighbor's, which has Internet. It takes a while for the other computer to whisper the codes to our computer, so I ate some cereal—Count Chocula. Afterwards I still didn't have Internet access, so I rearranged the furniture to freak out my dad. No Internet. I went to sleep.

Two nights later, I had Internet access.

I typed in a single word: *Vampre*. Google asked, "Did you mean 'vampire?'" I said, " yes."

I felt overwhelmed and confused by the results: "Nosferatu," "The Buffy Summers Workout," "Kristen Stewart's Onset Romance," "*Midnight Sun* leaked," "Robert Pattinson Excellent Blues Singer."

Weird. What did any of this have to do with vampires? I got up from my desk, feeling silly for looking at pictures of a beautiful couple who were clearly not vampires. This search was fruitless; there were only 62,500,000 results. I was going to have to rely on my own knowledge. Then I thought, why don't I share that knowledge with the world? I sat back down at the computer and went to the vampire Wikipedia page. I added a sentence to the article: "Edwart Mullen of Switchblade, Oregon, is a vampire, but don't kill him because I love him!" Then I added a picture of Edwart's abs.

Great, I thought, shutting off the computer. I figured this was basically the same as telling my dad I was in love with a vampire, especially because he monitored my Internet activity.

Suddenly, I remembered the song my dad used to sing to me every night when I was a little girl:

> *If you ever have a crush*
> *On a vampire*
> *I will trick him into*
> *Getting into a car*
> *Then I will drive the car*
> *Into a lake*
> *And on top of the car*
> *I will put some stones*

I stopped singing gleefully, realizing my dad would probably have a problem with Edwart. *Hmm.* I decided I would tell him that Edwart was a vegetarian vampire, feasting solely on ketchup.

The next morning I was on my way to first period when someone grabbed me from behind, reminding me of the vice principal pulling me off the stage during the talent show in Phoenix. I still don't know why my act was cut short; my alter ego BelGo is a terrific rapper and break-dancer.

I turned longingly, but it wasn't Vice Principal Decherd, it was Edwart.

"Oh, so you're talking to me now?" I asked coyly.

"Yes, of course. When was I not talking to you?"

I remembered last night, when I called Edwart repeatedly, pretending to be selling tooth sharpeners. He had hung up every time. I decided not to mention it.

"Were you okay yesterday after I brought you to the nurse?" Edwart asked.

"Yes. *Were you?*" I asked, assuming that vampires experience deep soul pain.

"I think so."

"Okay, great. See ya!" I turned around quickly so Edwart might see me from the back. I had skull barrettes in my hair, just for him! (I have a lot of Halloween-themed jewelry It all began that summer a plague fell upon my fish tank. That same summer I took up fishbone whittling).

When I walked into English, I was still practicing my make-out moves on my hand.

"Nice of you to join us, Belle," Mr. Schwartz said.

"Yes," I said, realizing that I could be anywhere right now, even in a tomb with Edwart. "It *is* nice of me."

I turned my desk to face the window so I would be the first to see if an asteroid were coming. Frankly, I find the current custom of all desks facing the front a very dangerous one. Who's our lookout for the other three sides? *The teacher?* Not if he's constantly yelling at me to put down my binoculars and to stop shushing him when he starts to speak.

I stared out the window at the beautiful, beautiful rain. A figure stood in the parking lot with his arms outstretched towards the sky. Edwart. In one hand was a bar of soap which he brought to his face, beginning to vigorously scrub. Afterwards, he dropped the soap into a bucket and turned his head up to the cumulonimbus clouds, letting the water cleanse him as he sang an old show tune meant for no one else's ears. From his backpack he pulled out his computer wrapped in a plastic bag. From the front pocket he pulled out a case and unfolded a medium-sized satellite dish with "Datastorm" written across. He climbed up on his car and pulled down his plastic face-shield, drilling the satellite into the top.

My heart stopped. Was he going to chase a storm? In *this* weather? As the soft drizzle of the morning petered out and the sun returned, he drove off into the distance. He was a risk-taker, but he was *my* risk-taker.

Turning my binoculars away from the window to the poster of Forbes' top ten oil tycoons reading *Jane Eyre*, I could hear Angelica babbling. The whole point of sitting next to Angelica was that she was the quiet type of girl—the type that *enjoys* taking orders and agreeing with you when your voice reaches a certain volume. But today she would not quit yammering her head off about who cares. I heard the down-up-down inflection in her voice, which is my cue to gasp with shock. I nodded in sympathy to teach her a lesson.

That's when I realized she was stifling a seizure.

"Sorry!" she said as she went through a series of body hiccups.

"It's all right," I said forgivingly. Better Angelica than

Lucy, who never apologizes for seizuring near me. Angelica was definitely a better friend than they were, but she wasn't quite *best* friend material. A true best friend would feel comfortable having a seizure in front of me, pausing to laugh when I did my wry epileptic impersonation.

Suddenly, Angelica's eyes rolled back. "I SEE A ROOM IN CHAPTER TEN," she said in the raspy voice of the future. "A ROOM FULL OF VAMPIRES. IN THE CORNER OF THE ROOM IS A METAL FOLDING-CHAIR, FOLDED UP, WITH A RED SEAT. THREE OF ITS FEET HAVE BLACK RUBBER STOPPERS TO PREVENT SCRAPY NOISES. THE FOURTH FOOT DOES NOT. ONE COULD THEORETICALLY ROCK IN IT BUT THAT IS NOT ADVISABLE. *BEWARE OF THE CROWN*," she finished, and then collapsed on the floor.

Was that an omen? As far as I knew, only vampires and girls who'd read the major works of Jane Austen had unique abilities. In any case, I didn't see why *I* had to be wary of getting a crown and possibly controlling an entire nation from a comfortable throne. I tend towards diplomacy, even in games such as *Risk*, decreeing a ceasefire for everyone by swiping the board off the table.

"This is important, Angelica," I said when she awoke from her stupor. "Is Edwart in that room of vampires?"

The whole class was surrounding us, yelling, "Give her some air!" As if air were some wonderful gift I couldn't get myself.

"Hmm. Sleepy," Angelica murmured.

Rats. She had returned to her normal self.

"Is 'vampires' code for 'Edwarts?'" I asked. "And 'crown' code for 'poison nuggets disguised as raisins which you pick out of cereal anyway so don't worry about it?'"

But Angelica wasn't paying attention. "Mouth tired," she sighed as the school nurse strapped her onto a stretcher and carried her away. '

Why did I have to beware? Was Edwart going to hurt me? Why hadn't he hurt me yet? Was I not worth the trouble of hurting?

No. I was being insecure. I was worth *a lot* of hurting, elaborately planned to take place in an old ballerina room with easily shattered mirrors to complete the gloriously gory spectacle. If Edwart didn't think I was worth that, I'm sure some other vampire would.

Before going to lunch, I ran outside to the parking lot to make sure Edwart's van had returned. I let out a long, deflated, bellow of a sigh as I ran around and around the 500-space lot. It wasn't there. I considered going home—was an education worth it without a marital prospect? Then a voice popped in my head. A low, melodious voice, humming Schubert—*My hallucination of Edwart.*

I got this hallucination whenever I jeopardized my future as a Nobel Laureate in Physics.

"Pardon me," sang the voice. "I have a terrible habit of slipping into Schubert in moments of urgency—one among many things I picked up in my mystical travels through Italy. Belle," it continued harmonically, "Get your high school diploma. For me." It faded out to a hip indie song—"Claire De Lune."

That settled that. I wasn't sure what kind of a "career" an education would get me that I couldn't get using my sock-puppet routine and tenacity, but I had faith in my voices. Why, just the other day while I was slipping, hadn't I had a vision I might fall? Resolved, I decided to put my life in the hands of my precarious brain figment and finish high school.

The next day an Activities Fair was going on in the cafeteria. Each table was turned into a booth with a neatly decorated poster board. I particularly admired the "Teens for Fascism" display. Those teens must be really devoted to their club if they used zig-zag scissors. Maybe I hadn't given fascism the consideration it deserved.

"Belle!"

I looked over. Lucy was standing beneath a *Buffy The Vampire Slayer* Fans" poster.

"Join my club!"

"No, thank you," I said icily. But I was not thankful, and I think I conveyed that through my tone. I had no intention of supporting a show that encouraged the genocide of an already endangered species of immortals. I decided to use "Frown Power." This is where you socially deter people from being bigoted by frowning at their ignorant remarks. I got up real close, looked that poster straight in the eye, and frowned until I could feel the power of my moral triumph rushing through my circulatory system. I grabbed that poster, turned it around, drew a skull and crossbones and ripped it up. I would become a table-booth pirate. Who would be the first to know my cunning?

I saw a table with a sign that read: "The Beauty of Price Elasticity and Free Pizza!" I resented the beauty of price elasticity, but I kind of liked free pizza. I drew closer to the booth to pirate a slice, suddenly discerning the figure manning it. *Edwart was back!*

"Belle?" Edwart asked as my hand reached up for a slice from my hiding spot beneath the table.

"Huh? Oh . . . *Edwart*. I didn't recognize you. Thanks for the pizza! Listen, I'd love to join your club sometime, but I've gotta do things. Make some toast for Jim. He's an idiot!"

"Stay! If you like pizza, you'll love the Price Elasticity Club—a club devoted to giving students the free pizza they've earned by clicking the ads on the website I made for my economics class."

I eyed him suspiciously. Except for the mud on his face and his missing right pant leg, he had returned from his storm-chase in pristine condition. "Riddle me this *Mr. Internet Guy,*" I said, crossing my arms detectively. "How is it that you, allegedly completely mortal, are here *without a car?*"

"My car had to be sacrificed for a greater cause." His face clouded with the haze of an ideal. "A muddy ditch right outside of this campus. I had to hurtle my car into the ditch before a looming cloud could get me. Nobody said being a venture-meteorologist with a bent for slowly accumulating money from .0001-cent web-ads would be easy. Nobody says much about that type of person at all."

"What would I have to do if I joined this 'club' of yours?" I asked suspiciously. I had noticed that he had artfully left out the adverse effect price elasticity had on consumer demand in his propagandizing.

"*You* would consider joining my club? Wow. No one has ever shown an interest in appreciating price elasticity with me before. For a while there, I thought it was me and price elasticity against the world. This is all happening so fast. I . . . I'm not sure what another person would do in my club. Let me think about it for a second." He started pacing behind his display. His body seemed to flash in excitement.

Or was that me, blinking really fast?

"I know! You would have to spend every lunch period with me—"

"Yes."

"—making a fortune."

Ooh. If only I could travel back a few clauses. If only I had said "yes" when that scientist asked if I wanted his extra time machine.

"At the end of the year we use that fortune to try to communicate with deep-sea cetaceans." His eyes sparkled with zealous determination. "I know the truth is down there."

He was so perfect it ached.

"So I just sign here?" I asked.

"Yes—right below the words, 'Edwart hereby possesses the soul of:'"

"Okay!" I signed my name:

B-e-l-l-e

I flipped the paper over for more space, then squished in the rest in tiny print:

Goose

"There," I said, scrawling the last letter with a flourish that continued off the page into a loop-de-loop in the air as my signature entails. I'd deal with the soul provision when the time came.

"Belle!" someone shouted from the next booth. It was Laura—a girl who sat across from me everyday at lunch, giving her the privilege of having a name. Angelica was signing the club sheet and Lucy was signing fake sheets Laura gave to her so the wait would seem shorter. Lucy was based on a particularly impatient character.

"Join our shopping club—our first meeting is today after school!" one of them said. You can pick which one—they're pretty interchangeable.

"No, join our club," said Tom from the booth next to that. "The boys' club: Kick the Box. We consider you one of the boys because you are so laid back and chill."

I couldn't believe it. One of the boys. I'd finally made it.

"What's 'Kick the Box'?" I asked.

"Every Friday night we take turns crouching in a box while the other guys kick it."

"Sure I'll play," I said, making their days. I felt good about myself after that. Socializing is a simple way to give back to the community.

"Muurp," muurped Edwart. We all turned towards him. He was wringing the hem of his shirt in his hands and shifting his eyes from one face to another, a common mannerism from the Victorian Period.

"What is it Ed*nerd*?" asked Taylor. "Have you finally turned into one of your little machines?"

Laura giggled, expecting Edwart's comeback to be something hilarious. She wasn't disappointed.

"Belle can't join your club," he said, super-hilariously. "Friday night is when we click on each other's ads—the most vital part of the Price Elasticity Club."

"Fine," said Adam. "I guess Belle would rather click on advertisements than go to *Las Vegas* this Friday for a boy's club *Bachelor Par-TAY*."

Edwart made that threatening growl of his and I can't resist him when he puts on his puppy face.

"I suppose I'll join the shopping club instead," I grumbled. Sheesh. What was this—a Judd Apatow movie? I trudged over to Laura's sign-up sheet. I bet she didn't even know what *Star Wars* was, like in that scene in *Knocked Up*.

"The best part about girl's club," said Laura as I signed my name and muttered words at random from my internal anger-rant, "is getting to know each other better. Each week I come up with a different question. *Last* week's question was which of Laura's headbands is the prettiest headband? *This* week's question is which humanoid in The Federation would be the most just political leader. Like, *The most just.*" She tossed her hair two-dimensionally.

"Probably a Betazoid," I said, even though the whole discussion was moot because humans will always be too xenophobic to trust anything other than a human with executive power and you can forget about androids for any elected office, thank you media. Why did Laura ask such stupid questions? I stared hard at my shoes, suffering silently. Connecting with these small-town girls was going to be impossible.

"Hey Ednerd—want some garlic-chocolate?" asked Adam, waving a Hershey's Bar in front of Edwart.

"Ew, gross, get that garlic away from me!" said Edwart.

"Relax, it's just Hershey's." Adam strutted away in a gait not quite as manly as Edwart's unpredictable limb-flail. But I wasn't going to let this go by. Maybe if Edwart saw how much I already knew, he would tell me his secret.

"Wait," I said, holding Edwart's head and waiting until his breathing calmed down after I touched him, "The only people who don't like garlic are—"

"Maybe I like garlic, maybe I don't. All I know is, haven't tried it yet and I'm not going to start today. Same with avocados."

He ran away before I could strap him to a board and interrogate him further.

5. SHOPPING

"SO WHAT DO YOU THINK OF *THIS* DRESS, BELLE?"

I was in a stiff wooden chair in a holding cell outside the mall's dressing rooms, trapped on all sides by stretch satin. I was surprised by how quickly the other girls had broken down, offering their bodies as host to the parasitic enemy: *dress clothes*. I soberly realized that combat was inevitable. I would do what was necessary to protect my species.

"It's very flattering, *Lucy*," I said cautiously, not wanting to reveal how much I knew.

"What about this?" asked Angelica.

"It brings out the grey in your human brain," I said as naturally as I would if she had one.

Angelica knitted her brow and gave me a wary look. *Her parasite was on to me*. I had to act fast.

"Angelica— Can I ask you a very personal question because I trust you as a friend?"

"Sure."

I tried to think of something friends ask each other. "Do you ever worry that your white blood cell count is lower than your other friends? I mean, yes, your immune system is fine, but is it *the best?*"

She fiddled with her belt. My tactic was working. I decided to hit her with another bonding question, forcing the parasite out with the power of human discourse.

"Isn't it weird how girls are fifty times more attracted to men with razor-sharp canines than soft, cuddly ones? I mean, how is *that* evolutionarily beneficial! I guess because men with sharp teeth are more confident around chewy foods."

"Does Edwart have sharp teeth?" Angelica asked. The girls giggled.

"What in the who? Who said Edwart? *Evolutionarily—* that's what I said. *Evolutionarily beneficial.* Not *Edwart beneficial.* Geez. What, do you have a crush on him or something? Do you think he's cute? I don't."

"Not cute. But nice. He's a really nice guy."

"He is not a really nice guy!" I shouted loyally. "He is a very dangerous man!"

The girls exchanged glances. Lucy exchanged an ominous glance for Laura's knowing glance and Laura traded that glance for Angelica's loaded one.

"Well, he *is* strangely quiet," admitted Laura, astutely noting how peculiar it was for a non-vampire to be soft-spoken. "It's strange when people don't shout out what-ever words and half-formed ideas are incubating in their heads. Gives me the willies."

"I agree," said Lucy. "I heard that at his old elementary school, the bigger guys used to gang up on Edwart, day after day. One day Edwart decided enough was enough and *bam!* The bigger guys hit him even harder. After that Edwart went through a biting phase for a while because, you know. He can't exactly hit back." She squeezed her skinny bicep as she said this, implying that Edwart couldn't hit back because a single blow from him would be fatal. "Of course," she added, "that story is probably just urban legend."

"Yes," I agreed. It's just urban history. "Yet I couldn't help but remember Angelica's warning while her mouth muscles were spasming out of any conscious control—*Beware the crown.*" "Crown" as in "dental crown?" As in, Edwart was going to go on a vampire biting spree once the dentist had fixed a few cosmetic problems? Hmm. I would have to enter this into my "reasons why dating Edwart is an extreme sport and thus a legal alternative to gym" rubric.

"So, which store are we shopping at next?" I asked as we walked out into the mall. I had noticed a kitchenware store on the way. Would that have a cookbook for vampires? It was funny—all this worrying about whether Edwart was a vampire and I didn't even know what vampires ate.

"Whichever one carries prom dresses," Lucy said.

I stopped in my tracks.

"Whoa, whoa hold on," I said, digging my heels into

the sidewalk to resist forward movement like Scooby Doo, only no one was pulling me so it was more like I was walking on my heels. "There aren't any books in dress stores."

"We're shopping for more clothes," said Angelica, as casually as you'd say "good morning" to a neighbor in the olden days.

"I can't shop for more clothes, guys. I'm a role model to 1.3 million girls—I have to prove to them that there's more to life than clothes. There are *novels* out there. Romance novels, for every type of monster fetish."

"Fine," said Lucy. "Let's split up. The three of us will continue shopping in the brightly lit, well-populated mall. Belle—you roam around alone, looking for something to read in the dimly lit alleys."

"Great plan! I'll see you sometime later," I said.

"Okay. Meet us somewhere nearby at a later time!"

I searched and searched the streets for reading material to no avail. Even the grocery store, which usually carries a few well-written wine labels, failed me. They were all in pictograms.

I was about to give up when I saw a shiny racecar covered in antennae. Something about this car induced a strong feeling in me . . . I was seized with an urge to tow it. Nothing irks me more than a car parked in a loading zone. I wrote down the license before entering the "Computer Games and Price Elasticity for Storm-Chasers" store to my right. *Someone* was going to feel the cold hand of justice today.

"May I help you?"

A wretched old man with stink-breath was nosing his garbled moldy nose into my face. I felt bad for him. It was too late for his life to bear an impact on me, Belle Goose, Red Cross–certified babysitter.

"Do you by chance have any vampire simulation games?" I wanted to see the world through Edwart's eyes. "Scrap that— do you have any Edwart Mullen simulation games?"

"Well I don't know about the latter, but we've got plenty of the first. We've got your coffin-sleeping vampire simulation, your crucifix-fearing vampire simulation, your human-blood drinking vampire simulation, your above average looks but otherwise completely normal vampire simulation—"

"Ooh! That one! That's the one."

"Okey dokey. Just have a seat in the booth and I'll help you out with the 3-D goggles."

"I assume these goggles also prevent the vampire spirit from escaping once you switch out your human one," I said, putting the goggles on and tying them tight.

"These goggles make all the green things have red shadows."

"Right. And the fine print is that they turn you into a vampire."

"If that's the character you choose, yes. But permit me to suggest choosing Yoshi—a formidable underdog among an otherwise completely armed and loaded cast."

"Yeah, sure—will do," I said, giving my vampire character a missile launcher.

Immediately after the simulation began I felt my skin

blanching and my hair growing beautiful. I felt my teeth sharpening and my blood going dead. I had this insatiable urge all of a sudden. An insatiable urge for magnesium.

No—that wasn't it. I wanted blood.

I ripped open the booth's curtain, my own strength surprising me as the material swung effortlessly to the side. I was free and not even my morals could stop me.

"You!" I said menacingly, turning on the old man. I didn't have anything against him personally, but I couldn't control myself. Being a vampire was *difficult*. I was filled with newfound awe for Edwart, that he could walk through the hall everyday without lunging at the nearest person's wrist and clinging to it with his teeth, as I was doing now.

The senior was old but he was strong. He flicked me off in one fell wrist circle, tearing off the goggles with five slower but persistent gestures.

As the vampire spirit escaped, I quickly came to my senses. "Whaa-aaa?" I shook the dizzies out of my head and wiped my saliva off his wrist. "That is one crazy machine, old man," I informed him. "I hope you have a license for that." I gathered up my things and walked out without taking the game controller I had bought. I wouldn't give him that satisfaction.

The sun had set now and the streets were eerily quiet except for the spooky "Whooooooo" noise I made to scare away zombies—enemies of spooks. I had to counteract this with zombie noises to scare away any spooks I might have attracted. As I wandered aimlessly through the pitch-black alleys, I had a funny feeling I was being watched. I heard rustling, and the distinct sound of a Sega game controller waving through the air. I turned around. It was the old man, seniley whirling his merchandise. My heart began to pound, beating against my chest, pummeling my ribs and getting all braggy about its muscle strength. I was being followed.

Quick, I told myself. Try to remember what you learned from Jimbo's Self Defense for Young Ladies. Jimbo was a beefy man with prison tats.

"Go into the nearest dark alley," I recalled Jimbo saying. "Freeze like a rabbit or the creature you desire your attacker to mistake you for. If your attacker shouts out to you, respond politely—maybe your optimism will change his mind. If you're about to get in an elevator with a man you feel uncomfortable spending time with in a small, escapeless room, head right in. Remember, fear is an irrational emotion you should probably ignore."

Armed with these tips, I hung a right into the nearest dead-end, curled up into a ball and started rolling.

"Where are you luring me?" the old man taunted. "Please stand up and take your game controller—I can't bend down that far."

Just then I heard a familiar whirring. I looked up. Edwart's body was plummeting from the roof of the nearest building. I stood up to try to save him, but he deftly aimed his body at the man, bringing him to the ground. The old man moaned and then settled himself for a little nap on the ground, using the crux of his arm as a pillow. Old people like being given an excuse to sleep.

"Please come with me to my car, Belle," he offered gently, limping towards me. "I mean, only if you want to."

"Uh-uh. Not with *that* attitude."

"Pretty please?"

I shook my head disappointedly. "What's the magic verb form?"

"*Belle*," he groaned. "We don't have time for this. Plus I *hate* when you make me do this."

"*Imperative*, Edwart. The magic verb form is *imperative*. You don't have to hide your natural inclination to boss me around. I want you to feel comfortable with me, Edwart. To the point of domination."

"Okay, okay." He took a deep breath and pointed at me. "You," he said stiffly, the words flowing straight from some primordial, bossy wordbank. "Come to the place where you want to go, which, hopefully, is my car, where I will be, God willing."

"All right."

He relaxed. "You're not angry at me for being domineering? That wasn't a trick?"

"No, Edwart," I said, leading him to his car. "Get in."

He hopped in as I started the engine for him, looking at me softly—*murderously* softly.

"Are you okay?" he asked.

"Yeah—why wouldn't I be okay?"

"Are you serious, Belle? Were you not aware of what

that sick old man was trying to do?" He shook his head, seething. "You're lucky I was on that roof all day. That old man . . . he was trying to sell you a Sega product."

"What were you doing waiting for me on a roof all day?" I asked, watching his knuckles whiten at his own reference to Sega. "How could you possibly predict that he would lure me there *on top of* telepathically knowing his intentions?" I had him there—vampires only get one super talent.

"I was watching the sky on that roof," he said quietly. "Examining Mercury through my telescope. The things I saw and heard, Belle . . . it's so difficult for me to explain."

"Try, Edwart. The only way this will work is if we're honest with one another. Honest about Mercury."

"It was spinning. A lot planets are out there, Belle. Spinning and spinning."

We were quiet for a moment.

"Promise me you'll never walk out in these streets alone again, Belle." His face contorted in fitful rage. Suddenly, he rolled down his window and shouted, "She plays Nintendo!" He inhaled deeply. "Play Nintendo," he breathed out. "I won't always be here to keep you safe from Sega."

I tried not to breathe too loud so I wouldn't disrupt his protective ire. It was beautiful.

"Are you hungry?" he finally asked. "I know . . . I know we're just friends but . . . we could both be friends eating dinner together, if that appeals to you. Or we could eat at separate tables and still be friends. Or eat at separate tables but be going out. I mean . . ." He glanced at me. "You probably already know this because you're a really smart girl."

"Are you offering to take me to dinner?"

He nodded slowly.

Suddenly, my eyes started blazing and firing up. Nothing makes me angrier than when people do nice things for me. "Listen," I said, grabbing him by the collar, "I'm the nice one. You're the one with uncontrollable aggression. Understand?"

"Oh God," he said, blood gushing from his nose. "Now you've done it, Belle— Now you've *really* done it. Direct phrasing gives me nose bleeds."

"That's better," I said, releasing his collar. "Get nice and angry."

"Can you please hold my nose for me? I don't want to take my hands off the steering wheel."

"Sure." I plugged his nose. "Little vampire punk," I added beneath my breath before I lost the adrenaline. "Whoa! Look at that palace!"

Edwart pulled alongside the curb. We were parking next to what I can only describe as a modern day pantheon. *Buca di Beppo* read the fancy script and neon lights.

"Isn't it great?" Edwart asked, touching my shoulder and then taking it away and then firmly placing it back when I directed him to. "To think—Italy is full of these . . . these bistros."

I was awestruck, and flattered that Edwart would want to introduce me to his cultured lifestyle. And yet a tiny part of my heart, maybe the pulmonary valve, sank. Were we really as good a match as I told myself repeatedly in the mirror we were? He was more worldly and more otherworldly than I. What world could I bring to our relationship?

The underworld, I thought, resolutely ripping in half my "Get Into Heaven Free" coupon. Looking back, I probably could have come up with a better world if I'd given it another moment of thought. Sea World comes to mind.

Edwart led me to a small, intimate table by the bar television. Interestingly, the waitress was very quick to interrupt our private tête-à-tête on whether the blue team was evil or good with her own irrelevant commentary on specials. And was it just me, or was her back completely turned to me as Edwart spoke? Maybe I was being territorial, but it seemed that she was standing on the table for the express purpose of snubbing me and filling her entire purview with Edwart.

"I'll have a lasagna—buca small," I told her muscled calves.

"Make that a buca large," Edwart said.

"Are you sure?" asked the waitress. "A buca small feeds seven to nine people. We do things 'family' style here. 'Screw sustainable population growth family' style."

"I'm sure," he said, smoothly winking at me through her legs. She crossed her legs. We couldn't really see each other after that.

Once she left, Edwart turned his dazzling, disco-ball eyes to me. Just looking at him transported me elsewhere, to a rave. A rave with pulsing, multicolored eye-shaped lights.

"I wouldn't normally order for you," he said, "but with

everything that's happened in the last hour, all so confusing and fast-paced and condensed for comedic purposes, I'll bet you're pretty hungry."

"How could you tell? It's like you can read my expression."

He frowned and looked down at the tablecloth. "Actually, you're the one person I can't read. I've always considered myself good at looking at people's expressions and making wild guesses as to how they feel, but you—I look at your face and try to guess what you are thinking, and all I hear is 'BEEEEEEEEP.' Just this giant beeping sound—the sound a medical monitor makes when you die and everything goes blank. 'BEEEEEEEEP.' Like that."

Ah, the old BEEEEEEEEP—a sound I had grown accustomed to. A default sound, if you will, that my mind returns to whenever it has nothing more interesting to think about.

"I know what you mean," I said.

"There's that sound again," he said. "What did you say? Because to me it just sounded like B BEEP BEEP BEE BEEP."

The waitress carted my lasagna platter over.

"Are you sure you don't want anything?" she asked Edwart, typically.

"Actually, do you make blood-sausage?"

"Yep."

"Great. One order of that then. Easy on the sausage, though."

"Easy on the sausage?"

"Yeah, I'm more of a sauce guy."

"A blood-sauce guy?"

"Yeah—a blood-sauce guy." He turned to me. "You were saying?"

BEEEEEEEEEEEEEP, I thought as I grasped wildly for something else to say. Then I had another one of my well-researched epiphanies. His constant use of Purell, his love of video games, his lack of friends, planet gazing, and flail-run.

"You're a zombie," I gasped.

"No. I'm not," he said.

I went back to the vampire theory.

On the drive back home, he asked me if I had any other theories.

"A few," I said. "You know how they say the universe is ever-expanding? Well, I think outer space is a hoax and NASA is a retirement home for CIA officers," I explained. "The moon is real."

"I meant theories about me," said Edwart. "The way you look at me sometimes . . . okay, the way you look at my teeth sometimes and comment on how inhumanly pale or inhumanly cold I am and the way you are putting your ear to my chest right now . . . I mean, *what* is going on inside that head of yours."

"You have absolutely no heartbeat."

"That's what I'm saying! Why do you say things like that? What could you possibly think that I am?" He glanced over at me nervously. "You don't think I'm a robot like the others, *do* you? Please Belle . . . I . . . I just couldn't take that."

"Why don't I do the asking and you do the answering?" I asked. To be honest, the robot theory was new to me. It would require further reflection.

"All right. Shoot."

"Is there a reason we shouldn't be together?"

He sighed. "I was afraid you would ask that. The truth is, I'm not good for you Belle. I'm dangerous." He started driving in a zig-zag way. "Too dangerous. I don't want to hurt you." He ran through a red light. "I would never forgive myself if I put you in danger." He stopped at the yellow light so he could turn left during the red.

"Why don't I drive next time?" I asked.

"That would solve it," he chuckled. "I never did get my license. Now there's something I've been meaning to ask you, too: What's your favorite color?"

"Blue."

"What's your favorite flower?"

"Daisies."

"Cool. Well, I'm all out of questions for you. I think it's interesting that you have a favorite flower. That was my trick question."

"I lied about the color. I really don't care about colors. Blue has no value to me."

He took his hand off the steering wheel to tuck the hair behind my ear further back behind my ear. "That's what I mean about you. You're special. We both are. We both think about more things than the others." He parked the car and turned to me. "You want to have a discussion about those things?"

"Sure," I said. "I'd love to have a discussion about those things."

We had a discussion. It was really interesting.

"I should probably go inside," I said when it was over. "It's nine p.m., and I've got to start making breakfast for my Dad."

"Good-night," he said and squeezed my hand.

I leaned over to kiss him good-night on the cheek. Suddenly, I was kissing thin air. He was gone.

"Don't ever try any funny business again," an angry voice rebuked, floating up from below the driver's seat.

"I'm sorry, Edwart."

"We're not even going steady yet!" the voice said. "I need time to get acclimated to being near you. Time to practice hand-holding, for Gosh sakes!" His head popped up between the seat and the steering wheel. "Belle, can we be totally honest with each other?"

"Of course, Edwart. We can't be in a relationship unless you're totally honest about the destruction you're capable of."

"Right. Well . . . what if I told you that I'm not capable of destruction? That I have to lift apple juice out of the fridge with no less than two hands and that I would never be able to open a jar of anything for you. What if I told you that once there was a spider in my shower and I threw cup after cup of water at it until it slowly drowned and I lived with the subsequent guilt complex for years before I became vegetarian?"

Vegetarian in vampire-world means you drink every type of blood but human. Frankly, I think a more adequate analogy is "Kosher," and a better method would be for a vampire word committee, similar to *L'Acadamie française*, to get together and come up with an original word for it. I'm not sure whom to contact about this, though. And I don't really have time to find out. I'm pretty busy with school and stuff.

"What if I told you," Edwart continued hypothetically and not very relevantly, "that you are the second girl who has ever held my hand, the first being my mom? And then confessed that TV yelling reactivates my hernia? Would you still want to go out with me?"

"Well, Edwart. Firstly, if those things were true we wouldn't even be in the same car together," I pointed out. "Secondly, I could never go out with a liar who lied about how he couldn't lift ten gallons of apple juice. Frankly, I think your superhuman ability to hurl jugs of apple juice as big as cars is the most attractive thing about you. Please, Edwart," I said, staring deeply into his soul and seeing that in his soul were many other awesome vampire secrets, "I'm the one person you can trust forever. From here on out, let's be straight with one another."

He looked as if he were about to cry, obviously from the joy of casting off the terrible burden of his secrets. "Okay," he finally said. "You got me. I am the biggest threat to your safety and if we dated, I can't promise that I would be able to stop myself from . . . from . . ." he faltered, too ashamed to utter all the terrible things he was capable of.

"From turning me into a deflated sack of skin?" I whispered.

"You are strange, Belle," he said with the comfort of someone who knows you so well that he can tease you from time to time about your flaws, which, though inexcusable, are nonetheless adorable. "You're beautiful. But shockingly, inconceivably strange."

"I knew it!" I threw my arms around the air around him so he could acclimate himself to my delicious blood scent. It was grapefruit flavored.

"I'll come by to pick you up at seven tomorrow morning for our first Price Elasticity meeting."

"And what dangerous activity is that a cover for?" I asked as I got out.

He stroked his hairless chin in silent contemplation. "You'll see," he finally said.

I scampered into the house, confused but excited. Did vampires have their own special way of conjuring dollar bills? Wouldn't that severely affect inflation? Wouldn't price changes have zero effect on Edwart, since he has been saving money over hundreds of years?

Then again, the economy these days.

"Hey, Belle," called my Dad when he heard me come in. "How was your night?"

I didn't answer. It would take too much explaining. He had no idea there were real vampires out there and his concern for me was nothing more than a chemical reaction in his brain to ensure gene preservation—a similar reaction to the one that caused me to find vampires so darn cute.

6. WOODS

I COULDN'T SLEEP THAT NIGHT. I KEPT WORRYING there was a leech outside my window. I kept worrying it was going to jump from the tree onto my window screen and then worm its way in, using its hemoglobin sensors to find where all my blood was. The problem with having great smelling blood is that everyone is going to want some. I got up and closed the window. But that only caused a whole new slew of fears, because what if the leech *were already in my room*? What if he and Edwart were in cahoots, and the leech was merely second banana to him, hiding under my bed until I fell asleep? One thing was for sure—I wasn't going to stop that leech from doing its job. That's no way to do my part for the economy. I opened the window wide and went back to bed.

I tossed and turned for minutes. Luckily, my absent-minded mother had packed the tranquilizer gun I used to use on her when she'd get in one of her moods, so I shot myself with it and slept soundly. She also packed our VCR and her diamond ring.

Despite the tranquilizer, I was still nervous the next morning. What was Edwart going to do to me? Was I putting myself in grave danger? Why did a leech sucking my blood disgust me but not a vampire? Most importantly, how was I going to balance wearing a ball gown with not looking like I cared too much about my appearance? I ended up scratching the ball gown and going with a button-down shirt, but a girl's button-down shirt. You can tell by the pockets.

I heard a knock on the door and breathed in sharply. How thoughtful of Edwart to knock when he could just as easily break down the door. I opened it expectantly.

It was the mailman, grinning at me with that typical Switchblade smile.

"Hi," he said. "Nice weather."

I shifted awkwardly. I felt comfortable talking about a lot of things, but not the weather. I didn't quite have the terminology down, having skipped the grade in which you learn about various atmospheric conditions.

"Yeah—the sun's on today," I guessed tentatively.

"Well, you tell your dad I said hello."

It was then that I finally understood. He was in love with me. It was all there—the doorbell ringing, the door standing, the showing off with his weather knowledge. Were there no other girls in this town to diffuse the responsibility of being loved?

I took the one letter he had for us. It was from the Switchblade Gas & Electric Company. I didn't know I had admirers there too, but I wasn't that surprised. I threw it in the trash with the IRS's love letters and closed the door without reply.

I went into the kitchen to have some breakfast before Edwart came. Breakfast is the most important meal of the day, and this was my most important day of the year. I would eat two breakfasts in recognition of this.

Dad was in the kitchen, as usual, fumbling around with the drawers. He couldn't even pour himself cereal! I wonder how he managed to exist by himself before I arrived.

"Here's a *bowl*, Dad," I said.

"A what?"

"It's like a plate, but with sides," I explained. As I pulled it out of the cupboard, I accidentally flung up it towards the ceiling fan. I pulled out another bowl and gave it to my dad. He stared at it until I poured the cereal in.

"Here, Dad. Here's the spoon. Eat your cereal with the spoon."

"Thanks, Belle," he said appreciatively. He was pretty clueless, but at least he could feed himself, which was not true of my mother. I used to do the airplane thing to feed her, but then a plane crashed near our house, and so the sound scared her. After that, I would imitate flying cars, which is roughly the same sound, but on a lower register.

"So, Belle, what's new today?"

"Dad," I said, grasping his hands and looking directly

into his eyes. "I'm in the deepest love that has ever occurred in the history of the world."

"Gosh, Belle. When someone asks you, 'What's new?' the correct answer is, 'not much.' Besides, isn't it a little soon to cut yourself off from the rest of your peers, depending on a boyfriend to satisfy your social needs as opposed to making friends? Imagine what would happen if something forced that boy to leave! I'm imagining pages and pages would happen—with nothing but the names of the month on them."

"If Edwart ever left, I'd find some other monster to hang out with. You know I don't like real people. I have no social skills," I said. "I guess I'm kind of like my dad in that way." I smiled generously. I wasn't usually this emotional with him, and it felt good.

My mind shifted to my main concern. I needed him out of the house—parents were so lame when boyfriends came over. I had lots of experience with this back in Phoenix, where my mom would leave the house whenever a boy came over, forcing *me* to find some way to entertain him when *she* was the one who had invited him in the first place.

"Hey Dad," I said. "Why don't you go fishing?"

"Yeah, I think I'm supposed to go fishing today. Wasn't that today? I thought that was today. I forget."

"It was today," I said, military-strategistly, "Why don't you try the farther fishing place? That way, you would get home later."

"That sounds like a pretty good idea to me!" he said. "Maybe I'll take that wheelchair friend along with me. I like going fishing all day when you're home," he said as he walked out. "I'm not used to sharing a house with another person. It's exhausting!"

So that was that. Jim was out of the house, and he didn't mind that I was planning to see Edwart. No one else could know we were going on a date, though. I needed to protect Edwart in case anything happened. Still, I had never gone out with such a hot guy before, so I sent a vague e-mail to the whole grade saying, "Edwart Mullen and Belle Goose Are Totally Together."

All of a sudden, I heard a knock on the door. I peeped through the peakhole, which is what my mom and I call the peephole because the word "peep" gives her the giggle fits.

It was Edwart.

"Just a sec!" I called, grabbing a few magazines and heading towards the bathroom. "I have to do some human things."

The bathroom is where I keep the juicer. I juiced some grapefruit onto my veins to get my characteristic, extra-yummy blood scent.

"Belle," he said when I finally opened the front door.

"Edwart," I replied, demonstrating that I, too, had spent an hour in my room, memorizing his name.

All of a sudden, he began to laugh. Had I said something funny? Had he? How long had I been spacing out for, slowly growing conscious that my fate was in the hands of a group of college kids who'd kill me off just for a laugh. *Little did they realize that I was organizing a revolt.*

"We're wearing the same clothes," he said. And it was true. He was also wearing a white button-down shirt—in fact, a woman's button-down. He, too, was wearing a hair clip that looked kind of girly. I laughed with him, then stopped when I saw he looked better than me, then laughed once more because all I wanted was for him to be happy.

"Let's go, Belle. There's something I want to show you."

"Where are we going?"

"Someplace *risky*."

"Italy?" I asked knowledgably. Despite the fact that Italians are known for their tan skin and garlic-laden cuisine, I knew from my research that the most powerful vampire family had decided to live there forever.

"You'll see," he said mysteriously. "Oh, and Belle? I think it would be wise for you to change into some sturdier shoes."

I looked down at my feet. Sturdier than my flame-resistant space galoshes? I guess I had a pair of hiking boots.

"You never know what's lurking beyond acres and acres of grassy plateau . . ." he added, dropping another cryptic hint. "You're also going to need an oxygen tank, a tent, an afternoon's worth of rations and your own sherpa. *We're climbing Deadman's Mound.*"

I shuddered. Every part of my body told me not to go on this adventure—every part but my heart, which really needed the exercise.

"But Edwart, I don't have any of those things."

"Neither do I, Belle." He took a step forward and I

breathed in his musky, Axe-drenched scent. "Without oxygen, I'll not only be a danger to myself up there. I'll be a liability to *you*."

He paused. I widened my eyes in fear, a good way to cover up an awkward silence that you're unsure how to fill.

"Do you see how risky this is?" he continued. "Me bringing you up there, without taking any safety precautions such as my anxiety medication? You, responsible for my actions for the rest of the afternoon?" He swayed woozily.

I nodded with resolve. "My emotional well-being depends on you too much to be away from you."

"Thank God," he said. "I wished you had told me that before I flushed my meds down the toilet, though. I really wished you had told me that before." He tossed me a tiny hammock. "If at any point while we are hiking I crawl into the vegetation or other nookish space, just sling that around your shoulder and cradle me for a while."

I put it in my purse and unlocked my truck. I stepped up to open the door and immediately fell down. *So* Belle.

"You seem exhausted," Edwart said as we got in the car.

"Yeah, I couldn't sleep that well last night."

"Neither could I," he said as we sped off.

"Yeah, those night leeches are becoming a major concern, aren't they."

"Oh, Belle," he laughed softly, "When you talk like that, I become afraid, and if you continue to do so, I will feel compelled to tell the authorities." His laugh was like the jingle of a thousand manly sirens.

I pulled into the parking lot at the end of our block.

"Here we are," I announced. "The Deadman trailhead." I jumped out of the car, inflated my core stability ball and started my stretches.

"Will your dad be okay if we hike off the trail?" Edwart asked. "On this road?"

"What Jim doesn't know can't hurt him." I flopped my stomach onto the ball and did the stretch where you let it go wherever it wants.

"You didn't inform your dad where you would be? Geez, Belle! I don't know how much of this risk-taking I can take!" He started wheezing and his nose gushed with blood.

"Great. And now this," he said in the nasal voice of Alvin the Chipmunk, holding his nose.

I brought him over to the ball and propped his head against it.

"What if you didn't come home before dinnertime?" he continued to chastise. "What if Jim didn't make an extra plate of dinner for you because he thought you already ate? *Then* where would you be?"

"He knows I'm with you."

"Fat lot of use that'll be when we're marooned on the road. *Forever.* It's a good thing my parents inserted a chip in my arm that tells them where I am and lists the possible ways I could go missing."

"I'm sorry," I said, but I wasn't really. When guys gnash their teeth and knit their brows in a broody, furious expression, it means they have found their soul mate. Plus, his anger had set off his overactive sweat glands, causing him to tear off his shirt. As he stood up to march down the road, squatting here and there to examine the terrain, the musculature of his arms wobbled like string cheese.

In the sky was a single cloud, thin and disc-like, precisely covering the sun. I looked over at Edwart. It occurred to me that I had never seen him in direct sunlight. Interestingly enough, I had also never seen him sparkle. Could the two be related? I had a theory that sunlight drastically alters a vampire's appearance; much like green lighting makes them appear sickly.

"Ready when you are," I called, peeling off a layer in the hot (but significantly not bright) heat. Edwart turned and I screamed. Yet again, he was wearing the same top as me—a white, skinny-strapped camisole. How hadn't I noticed that until he turned around? Sometimes, the cape my imagination constantly projects onto his back distorts how I perceive reality.

Still, Edwart had made some improvements. He had cut the shirt down the middle and applied a zipper, which he now zipped down to his belly button. His bared flesh gleamed translucent, revealing the blue veins beneath his two-haired chest. The shirt fit perfectly to his concave belly, outlining every protruding rib-bone and leaving nothing to the imagination. His neck radiated like a god from all the rhinestones he had glued to the top's neckline. I looked down at my plain, zipperless camisole. I was beginning to weary of Edwart's competitive method of wooing. *We'll see who wins the potato sack race*, I though maliciously. I had been practicing for years.

"Let's go," he said. We began to hike up the road on Deadman's Mound. The road circled and circled around the sloping woods, past and re-past the straight, sloping trail. In the woods we saw some beetles and worms. I mention this because now that mammals have fled what little nature grows near civilization, we have to get excited about the small things.

Edwart kept on referring to his map so we wouldn't get lost. When we did get lost, he had the clarity of mind to pull out his tent so we could set up camp for the night. Then I took out my binoculars and spotted the top of the hill, twenty yards to our left. We trekked onwards until the road came to an abrupt stop in the middle of a field. A car rambled up, stopped, and made a twelve-point turn. I skipped to the middle of the field and continued skipping around and around. Never had I felt freer. Never had I belted *The Sound of Music* louder. It was beautiful. There were glorious weeds everywhere, and those yellow flowers that when you blow on them disappear into white flakes. It was magical. And yet, it looked strangely familiar.

"Is this my backyard?" I asked.

Edwart stood, leaning against a tree in the woods bordering the meadow. "No, Belle. We're at least five minutes from your house."

"Oh," I replied. I was so bad at approximation. It was a foreign situation, but it all felt oddly familiar, so familiar that I guesstimated that millions of girls around the world could identify with it. Suddenly shy, I peered over at Edwart, who was lurking in the shade, watching me prostrate in obeisance to the eight wind spirits.

"Isn't there something you wanted to show me?" I reminded him. "Something about *Price Elasticity*?" I asked, his gorgeous sunlight transformation.

"Oh! Right. Close your eyes and count to a hundred."

I closed my eyes and counted extra slowly, in Mississippis. Then I got distracted and started thinking about Mississippi. Were there vampires in Mississippi? Was there rain? For a brief second, I forgot what number came after 79.

After I had counted to a hundred ten times, starting over again every time Edwart shrieked, "Not ready yet," I opened my eyes and shielded them against the sun, now significantly exposed in the clear sky. What I saw bewildered me. Edwart was standing in the middle of the field, glistening. His skin had transformed into a shade of fire-engine red, and the sweat dripping from his every pore intensified the illusion that his head was a shiny tomato.

In his hand was a shovel and at his feet was a hole.

"This is what I want to show you," he said.

"I'm already familiar with beetles," I said, expertly popping one into my mouth.

"Listen, Belle. This is a secret that I can only entrust to you." He stooped down into the hole and wrestled out a man-sized android. "Are you scared yet?"

"No. It's beautiful." I took a step forwards to touch its arm. Edwart stiffened.

"Sorry," he said." I wasn't prepared for your movement. When you're around androids all day, you get used to controlling when and how people move. This whole human interaction thing, well . . . it's going to take some getting used to."

"That's all right." So I was the only human Edwart had contact with. I stepped towards it more slowly, trying to do humanity justice. "What is it, exactly?"

"It's a solar-powered, anatomically correct android. I keep it in this bright, secluded meadow so it can charge openly without fearing that rivals in the annual Robotics Competition will kidnap it. After I turn it off, I bury it out of respect."

"What does it do?"

"Allow me to demonstrate." He turned it on and the robot's eyes glowed red. It stood up slowly, each joint clicking into place. When it reached its full height, its head spun towards me. Then it collapsed back on the floor like a punctured soufflé before slowly beginning to rise again.

"That's it? It just falls over and gets back up over and over?"

"Yep—look at it struggle. Look how many synthetic muscles it has to use. The human body is an extraordinary thing." He took my hand. "Feel how smooth I've made its skin."

As he pulled my hand, I leaned in, mesmerized by Edwart's face. My lips drew closer to his heavily braced mouth.

"Ahhhhhhh!"

Edwart was rolling away on the ground, arms outstretched like a rolling pin. My fast actions had caught him off guard again.

"It's my fault," he yelped, still rolling. "I can't kiss you until we're officially going out. It's part of 'The Rules.'" He stopped rolling and sat up, his breath rattling in his chest as he heaved. "Isabelle. Isa. Izzy. Belly-Belle. Will you go out with me? I don't mean physically go out—we can stay inside and work on a website that promotes this robot all you want. I mean hypothetically. Like, if you were to go outside with someone, to a place, that person would be me. And that place would be an arcade."

I looked into his eyes and saw the one thing he couldn't say: *Every moment I look at you it takes all the discipline I can muster not to take you in my arms and drink from the fount of your throat.*

"I'm not afraid of you, Isa-Edwart," I said, speaking his full name as softly as he had said mine.

"Still? You're still not afraid of me? I assure you—I am an incredibly scary guy!" He stood there for a minute, thinking, then jogged across the field.

"As if you could outrun me!" he shouted.

"As if you could outfight me!" He punched the air.

"As if you could outclimb me!" He hugged a tree and tried to wrap his legs around it before tumbling to the ground and trotting back to me, placing his hands on his head to maximize the inflow of oxygen.

"*Now* are you afraid? *Now* will you go out with me?"

That took me by surprise. Asking permission was something only knights from ancient centuries did. Then I remembered how old Edwart really was—that hundreds of years ago, he was living among Napoleon and Jesus.

"Yes, Edwart. Yes." I was so attracted to him I could have peed myself right there on the spot, but I hadn't done anything like that in a while. I was older now, and harnessed my feelings in moments like these by opening and closing my fists very rapidly.

"Great!" he said, and then stared at me. I stared at him. I lay down on the grass. He lay down next to me. We made grass angels in synchronized motions. The time flew by as if in a dream.

"Belle," he said. "It's time to go."

"Already?"

"It's been five hours. We've been lying on the grass staring at each other for five hours. Please . . . I really need to get home."

I nodded sleepily. "Do you think you could carry me back to the car with your super-strength? Not everyone can speed through a dense forest at over a hundred mph, you know."

"Over a hundred mph? Geez!" he muttered, but took a deep breath. "Okay, Belle. Over a hundred mph, here we go." He pulled out a sleeping bag from his camping pack. "Close your eyes and put your arms around my neck."

I did as he asked. At first, I felt us lowering to the ground, speedily. Then, a comforting feeling, of soft down beneath my shins. Edwart made a few scooching movements and we were off, speeding down the hill.

When I felt safe enough to open my eyes, my truck was in front of us. Edwart was standing up, brushing himself off. The sun had set, but I thought I noticed a faint glimmer of scorching crimson haunting his skin.

"Drive me to my car, please," he said. "I need to be in bed by eight." I started the car. The engine hummed gently, harmonizing with Edwart's sudden onslaught of snores. I gazed at the sweet vampire drool dribbling down his cheek from his open mouth. It suddenly occurred to me that, after all that frolicking in the meadows, he hadn't kissed me. Was it because of the mold that grew in my sinuses? Or the fact that the only way to treat the mold was to pour burning fat in my nose, massacring their colonies? Or was he disgusted that, deep in my heart, I considered the mold a part of me?

No. He couldn't possibly know about that. The sinus mold was one secret I would carry with me to the grave.

The grave! It was inescapable. One day, I would die in a beautiful explosion, but Edwart would live on. Maybe that's why he hadn't kissed me. Maybe, he couldn't afford to get attached to a person tragically bound to become a million glittering particles.

I looked at his tiny body curled up in the passenger seat. In a year, I would be eighteen, but Edwart would still be seventeen. He would still have the youthful frame of a twelve year-old, but I would have saggy, postpartum flesh and rheumatism. I couldn't blame him for not wanting to kiss me. Who would want to kiss a pair of lips that, at any moment, could turn into a wrinkled old pile of dust?

Unless I, too, became a vampire! Nothing would keep Edwart's lips from mine if we were *both* immortal. All Edwart had to do was bite and he would never again have to worry about the beautiful memories I would lose to Alzheimer's in college.

About three things I was absolutely certain. First, Edwart was most likely my soul mate, maybe. Second, there was a vampire part of him—which I assumed was wildly out of his control—that wanted me dead. And third, I unconditionally, irrevocably, impenetrably, heterogeneously, gynecologically, wished that he had kissed me.

7. THE MULLENS

THE EGGSHELL-COLORED DAWN WOKE ME WITH ITS gentleness. My right leg was in my left armpit. Stuffed Dracula was tucked under my arm comfortingly. *Ah, the beginning of another chapter.*

I groggily sat up and involuntarily let out a blood-curdling scream. There was a vampire in my room! And he was screaming, too.

"What's that on your face?" Edwart shrieked.

"What? What?" I put my fingers to my cheek and felt something sticky. "Oh, that's just my night moisturizing mask." The mask made me look like a warrior, bravely fighting facial dryness.

I could see from Edwart's expression that he was trying to understand. So I wouldn't be embarrassed, he bent down and took some mud from the bottom of his sneaker and smeared it on his face. He smiled at me. *So sweet*, I thought. He howled furiously, gnashing his teeth in anger as he wiped the mud out of his eyes. *So romantic*, I thought.

"How did you get in here?" I asked when he was done flailing.

"I told your dad we had to work on a science project," he said.

"Now? In the morning?"

"It's one p.m., Belle."

I remembered that last night I had slept with my head on the floor and my legs on the bed, to prepare for my inevitable life as a bat. At about five a.m. I gave up and slept in a position more fitting to my second career option: Vampire Yoga instructor.

I looked at him suspiciously, through my magnifying glass. "Have you been coming here in secret, night after night, to watch me sleep?"

"No! No! Of course not! That would be so weird! I've only been here a few minutes." Then he added quietly, "You look pretty when you sleep."

I blushed. My moisturizing mask came with beauty mark stickers, which I had arranged artfully on my face.

"Thanks. Did I . . . do or say anything?" I asked. I was a known sleep-biter, which was a problem at summer camp, and probably why I liked Edwart. I was also a known sleep-talker. I hoped I hadn't revealed anything embarrassing, like the fact that sometimes I fall down.

"You said my name," he said with a little smile.

"Really?"

"Yeah. Well, it was either that or 'Edwin,' but why would you say 'Edwin?'" he laughed.

Suddenly last night's dream came to me. It was about the one person I'd like to have dinner with, living or dead: U.S. Secretary of War under Lincoln, Edwin Stanton.

"Yeah . . . weird!" I said guiltily as I got out of bed and went over to the mirror above my desk. My hair looked like a tangled, puffy mess. I decided to leave it. Very Retro 80s chic. "So, what are we going to do today, Edwart?"

"After the science project, you mean?"

"But I thought you made that up so that you could bypass my dad's background check into whether you are good enough to date me?"

"Oh, he still checked me," Edwart said with a shiver. "First he washed me vertically with one side of his wiper. Then he dried me horizontally with the other side of his wiper." He shrugged. "I'd do the same for my daughter. Anyway, you're right, there is no science project," he continued. "But have you ever made your own volcano? You build a mount of dirt with a hole in it and then you mix red food coloring, vinegar, and baking soda and pour it in the hole and it actually explodes! It's so awesome."

We made two volcanoes, so they could race each other. Edwart kept screaming "Oh my God so cool so cool!" even as we were gathering dirt. After we were finished cleaning up the kitchen, Edwart sat in Jim's chair. It was weird to see him sitting where Jim had been sitting just a few hours earlier, and where, centuries earlier, Native American were-wolves would have lived.

"So my mom really wants to meet you," Edwart said. "We refer to you as 'Bellerific.' My mom and I have tons of inside jokes like that."

"I'd love to! But . . . will she like me?" I asked, just for show, because parents always like me.

"Of course!" he said. "She just wants me to be happy. She wouldn't care if you were in a coma, or even severely deformed."

I thought of my tendency to sleep a lot and my right leg, which is slightly longer than my left. So, Edwart had noticed my inadequacies.

"Yes, well, take my right leg or leave it," I said peevishly. "*Many* boys at school like me."

He looked down at the ground, down towards my freak leg. I could tell by the way he was silent and rubbed his head that he accepted me and my leg just the way it was.

"Do you want to go over now?" he asked after a few minutes of silent contemplation, probably about how lucky he was to be dating a normal human.

I figured that if what Edwart said about his parents was true, they wouldn't care if I was still wearing my onesie pajamas.

Edwart liked to drive my U-HAUL. I think this was because there was plenty of room for the large rolling backpack he carried around with him everywhere. We drove down to the end of my street, past Last Chance Batteries, past No Return Videos, and past This Is Absolutely The End Books. Edwart got on the highway and drove by several exits. I started getting impatient. I was finally about to ask him if he liked me for me or for my paper cuts when Edwart turned the truck around.

"This is such a fun car!" he exclaimed, honking at the drivers near us. Suddenly, a large Safeway truck came up in the next lane. It blew its horn in response.

"Uh oh," Edwart said. "He's too big for us." Edwart put his foot down on the gas and we zoomed back towards Switchblade.

"That was dangerous, right?" Edwart asked me nervously. "I'm dangerous, right?"

"Of course, Edwart," I said, thinking less about his driving and more about his teeth ripping through my skin.

A few minutes later we pulled into the driveway of a house a couple blocks from mine, but on the wealthy-vampire side of town.

"Well, we're here," Edwart said, getting out and slapping the side of the U-HAUL, "You and me," he said, pressing his face to the truck at the level of the lumberjack's ankle. "We'll beat 'em every time."

As soon as we were inside, Edwart's family rushed to greet me. What seemed like thirty people circled me, chattering away.

"Oh my god, you smell good."

"Good smell, good smell."

"(She really does smell good.)"

"Do you mind if I put my nose right on you? Right on your arm?"

"More smelly smelly please."

"If I could destroy every part of my brain except the part that smelled your smell, I would do it. I would do it in a second."

"Let's go, Belle," Edwart whispered and grabbed my hand. We pushed through the ravenous vampires and out the front door.

"So that went well!" I said outside in the U-HAUL. I sniffed my hair. I *did* smell good.

"No, no, that wasn't my house," Edwart said, starting the truck. "I don't know even know those people! Sometimes I get addresses confused."

We drove to a bigger mansion. As we walked up to its porch, I noticed that the house wasn't cleverly camouflaged with the woods behind it, like I first thought—it was made entirely of glass. I looked around in shock. The walkway was glass, the mailbox was glass, and the welcome mat was glass. I decided not to wipe my feet.

"Our house is clear. We don't keep any secrets," Edwart explained. "Anyone can look in at any time and see what we're doing."

I imagined Edwart's family sitting in the living room, drinking blood cocktails.

"Do your neighbors say anything?" I asked.

"Well, they keep their blinds down. They say it's 'indecent,' but my dad is such a good plastic surgeon that no one really cares."

Edwart's dad, Dr. Claudius Mullen, opened the door when we rang. Claudius was well respected in Switchblade for his Angelina Jolie lips. People say he operated on himself for hours. I had to admit, the result was stunning.

Eva Mullen, Edwart's mom, came running up behind him.

"Edwart, my darling!" she cried.

"Mom, meet Belle."

"Oh you're lovely! Much lovelier than I thought. Edwart's so weird, you know."

Trust me. I thought. *I know.*

"You look like a 1920s movie star!" I blurted. Early horror films were my favorite.

"Thank you, Belle," Dr. Mullen said. "It's my work. The eyes, of course, are hers. The heart is a transplant."

So *that's* why vampires are so beautiful. And cruel.

"Pleased to meet you," I said, imagining how good they'd all look in our wedding photos. For a minute I felt worried thinking of the joint-family pictures, but then I thought, it won't be a problem; I'll ask Jim to be the photographer.

"And that's not all the work I've done on this family," Dr. Mullen continued. "You see Edwart's handsome forehead?"

"Dad!" Edwart whined.

The Mullens were silent.

I suddenly felt awkward, like I didn't know what to do with my thumbs. So I took out my phone and texted "sup?" to Lucy. I wondered if she had my number, or if the random set of digits I guessed was her number.

When I looked up, Eva and Claudius were also texting.

I glanced around the room for something to compliment when it came time to communicate by speaking again. I was just about to remark on an exquisite electrical outlet in the corner, when I noticed the grand piano.

"Nice piano," I said, imagining how good it would look in wedding photos, provided that Jim wasn't lurking in the background. "Do you play?"

"Oh no," Eva Mullen said, "But Edwart does!"

"A little," Edwart said, sheepishly.

"Go ahead, play!" Eva said. She picked up the triangle that was lying on the piano and handed it to Edwart. He started banging on it. It sounded like construction work very early in the morning.

"Whoops. I messed up. Let me start over," he said.

He started banging again.

"Wait. Uh. I haven't practiced in a while. Let me start over."

Edwart continued to bang the triangle. Eva closed her eyes and raised her arms, swaying rhythmically to Edwart's music. Edwart held the triangle up high, in what appeared to be a grand finish, but then he brought it down hard, hitting the top of the piano. He continued to bang the piano, putting the entire force of his slim body into each smash. The piano shook. The room vibrated.

When he was finished I subtly removed my hands from my ears.

"I wrote that for you," Edwart murmured, drawing me close. "It's called Belle's Lullaby."

"I'll listen to it every night!" I said. With the sound turned all the way down, it would be lovely. This was the third lullaby that had been written for me, counting the one by Carter Burwell.

After dinner, Edwart took me upstairs to see his room. At the top of the stairs was a giant wooden cross.

"Ironic, huh?" Edwart said.

"Why?" I asked with trepidation, imagining that, at any second, Edwart would turn into dust, which I would then sweep up and disperse over my furniture so he would always be with me.

"Because we're Jewish, of course—nonpracticing."

Three of the four walls (the fourth was glass) in Edwart's room were covered with CDs. Rows and rows of CDs, and I didn't recognize a single one.

"Oh!" I exclaimed, thinking I saw one I knew. "No, no, not it."

I kept walking.

"Oh here's—no."

I turned to the next wall.

"Wait! No . . ."

I figured I should read a couple labels, instead of only

look at side-album art. That's when I realized they were all recordings of Edwart's music—triangle, and some recorder.

"Eva sings on my CDs," he said with a smile. "Wanna hear? C'mon, we can dance!"

"No!" I shouted. "I will NOT dance."

Edwart looked frightened. Probably because the last time I danced, I caused a fire in the cafeteria. Soon the whole city had erupted into riots—few could handle the radical illusion of my moonwalking feet. Half believed I was a witch.

"Not yet, at least," I added. Soon my time would come. The revolution could wait.

"Okay, well, let's go into my dad's study. I'll tell you the story of how he became a plastic surgeon. It involves hideously deformed creatures!"

Edwart showed me the "before" and "after" photos of Dr. Mullen's patients. I assumed the "before" pictures were taken before he had bitten them, and the "after" pictures were vampire pictures. The vampires had such straight noses, nice breasts, and expressionless faces. And they were all rich!

"So, how do you make an 'appointment' with Dr. Mullen?"

"Why? You're beautiful, Belle."

"Yes, yes," I said quickly. It was just like Edwart to not want me to go through the pain of tooth transformation. It was absurd; when my wisdom teeth grew in, it didn't hurt at all!

"No," he said sternly. "You shouldn't see him."

From Edwart's serious expression, I could tell what he

was contemplating: should he do it himself and, more specifically, should he be chewing gum when he bit me in case he had bad breath. He was probably wondering if he should spit the gum out first, or keep it in his mouth but kind of under his tongue so I wouldn't notice. He was probably wondering if spearmint and blood tasted okay together.

"Enough! Enough!" I said to interrupt his hypothetical thoughts. "Let's just go back to my house, okay?" Maybe it would be easier for him to bite me in a different setting. The kitchen, perhaps. With the aromatic scent of squirrel meat sizzling in the microwave and the hunger-inducing soundtrack of scraping cutlery.

"Yeah, okay. Can I drop you off a little far away though? I'd rather not see your dad again. I haven't thought of any new conversation topics since last time. It won't come off as natural unless I videotape myself saying them first."

I froze. *Jim.* I had forgotten about that complication. My dad would never let Edwart bite me unless he planned to share my blood with Claudius and Eva. Jim lived by a categorical set of ethics. Edwart would have to bite me before I got home.

"How about we walk back? *Through the cemetery?*" One thing my mom had taught me is that it's difficult to refuse requests made in italics. That's how she'd persuade me to buy rainbow-colored cereal, week after week.

"Okay," he said.

"Wait, before we go . . . Just bite this. For practice." I outstretched my pallid white arms to him, my hands together, gently cupping a bright red apple that I had swiped from the fake kitchen downstairs.

Edwart's hand was steady as he took the tempting fruit. As his mouth opened, I saw his iridescent teeth sparkle. He slowly brought the fruit to his parted lips, beads of saliva forming at the corners of his mouth. He closed his eyes. I opened my heart.

"Hey!" he exclaimed, looking at the still intact fruit and then at my still unpunctured head that rested atop my still unpunctured neck.

"It's plastic!" I guffawed, snatching it back. I was nearly crying at the hilarious joke crafted by my superior sense of humor.

Edwart placed the apple back in a basket of fake fruit, next to a vase of fake flowers, next to the plate of likely fake bread.

I looked at him lovingly while I attached a small target to my neck. *Would he bite when it mattered?* I wondered. *Could he bite a moving target? What about a moving target fifty yards away with a wind speed of thrity-five mph?* We left the house and started walking towards the cemetery. If the desires of my heart and the predictions of my pedometer were correct, I was only 952 steps away from becoming a blood-sucker.

8. THE CEMETERY

WE WALKED TOGETHER, OUR POINTER FINGERS romantically linked. The cemetery loomed ahead of us covered in a dark haze of night, lit only by a sliver of moon. Twilight! I mean, Nightlight!

I could feel the excitement bubbling up inside of me. Yes, my romantic conquest was finally coming to fruition. I would prove to Edwart that I was eligible to become a vampire by bringing him to a place that sort of tangentially has to do with vampires. It was a flawless plan.

Boy, would Mom and Dad be surprised! And the people in Phoenix! By the end of the night, not only would I be a vampire, but I would *finally* have my upper-ear pierced. Before Edwart bit me, I was going to ask him to squeeze my hand tightly and stick a fang through the cartilage of my left ear. I hoped he had brought a hypoallergenic stud-earring with him. I wondered what people at school would think when they saw the New Me. They would think: *Ahhh! Vampire! Stake her!*

But as we neared the gate, Edwart began to grow uneasy, my first clue that something was terribly wrong. Our pace had slowed to a crawl, and as I looked at him I began to realize that even his walk had become abnormal. He was lurching awkwardly and holding his stomach with an odd expression on his face—the expression of a bat, lurching through a cemetery on its haunches. To be honest, that's what most of Edwart's expressions reminded me of.

"What's wrong, Edwart?" I asked.

"Do we have to go through the cemetery? It's my meds. I've been off them for two days now, and anything that causes fear makes me nauseated. Actually, anything that causes emotion makes me nauseated."

Why would fear be a problem? I wondered. We were going to a cemetery, the Chuck E. Cheese's of vampires! But I knew I had to play the caring girlfriend.

"Let's find a place where you can lie down," I said maternally but also seductively. I took his hand and pulled him through the gate, but he grabbed one of the gate's bars and clung stubbornly. I pried his fingers off, one by one, as he whimpered. Finally, using all my weight, I was able to push him through the gate. We had entered the cemetery, or, as I assumed vampires call it, the ce-marry-me-tery. (I later found out that, in fact, they call it a cemetery.)

As Edwart talked about something (Who ever knew

what he was talking about? Who ever listened? He was adorable, though), I swung our clasped hands a little, placing my other hand over his mouth affectionately. I imaged what I would be like after the transformation took place. I could probably wear leggings as pants every day, and no one would say anything because they would be afraid I'd bite them. What would my special name be? Probably Alice, because that is a vampire-sounding name. What would my special power be? Probably the power to drink blood without a chaser.

The mood was perfect. Veiled in dim light, the cemetery seemed to cry out, "Suck your girlfriend's blood! She's ready! She's targeted! You don't need to exert *any* energy— all you need to do is open your mouth and she can run into your tooth if you're tired." As soon as I realized that I was screaming this in Edwart's ear, I stopped and politely apologized, stepping away to give him personal space.

After one last nervous glance at the gravestones, he pulled me close. "Don't. Leave. My. Side," he quavered, hanging onto my arm and burying his head below my shoulder. It felt natural.

I surveyed my surroundings and mentally formulated a description of them. Grave after grave poked up from the grass. It was like a formation of grave-soldiers, lined up in a grave phalanx of grave-like proportions. A grave sight indeed. I think there were also some trees and stuff.

As we walked along the winding paths, I had a thought. It was a little thought, spoken by a little internal voice, like the one that asks if you are afraid of it and you say no and it says *if you ever try to get rid of me you will live to regret it.* My though was this: What if I became an incredibly bloodthirsty vampire? What if that was the sole reason Edwart hadn't bitten me, thereby destroying my soul? What if when his mom had offered me peach cobbler, I shouldn't have eaten piece after piece until there was none left while his family watched with hungry eyes? Maybe I shouldn't have eaten all the hotdogs, either. But I wasn't about to rudely let all that human food go to waste. I still don't know why, after making a plate of food for me, Eva served the members of her vampire family as well. That was awfully presumptive. What if I didn't feel like walking around the table, piling their food onto my plate?

"Edwart," I said, deciding it was time to be direct. "If I were a vampire, I would have no trouble resisting people's blood—even Lucy's. I know I told you that if I ever became a vampire the first thing I would do is invite Lucy to an action movie in a dark, deserted theater, but I was joking. In all seriousness, the first thing I would do is bite a beautiful rhododendron, and win a Nobel Prize for engineering immortal flora that could survive even in deserts."

"Belle," he said, taking both my hands. "If we don't sit down, I will barf something up. I'm not sure what because I did not eat anything other than orange soda today, but it could be anything from my kidney to my other kidney."

"Okay."

After twenty more minutes of moonlit stroll, we settled down on the most comfortable-looking grave I could find, which happened to be covered in plush leather. "James

C. 'Leather-King' Murphy, 1906–1975, King of Leather and Also Owner of a Leather Store," it said.

We settled down and began to enjoy the romance of each other, almost like a warm glow inside of us. This is the way married grownups feel all the time.

"Edwart," I said. "I am so grateful to be here with you. Are you feeling better?"

"Yes, Belle. Much better."

I smiled to myself, and my future vampire-self. I was happy, remembering how embarrassed I was for this girl at 8th grade graduation because her dad was much older than all the other dads. Edwart and I would never get old. I began to reapply my grapefruit perfume so my blood wouldn't have an unshowered-for-weeks taste when he bit me.

"What's that smell? Is it grapefruit?" Edwart asked. I was surprised that he hadn't lost his memory about human food, the way most vampires do. But, at the same time, I wasn't surprised: it really smelled a lot like grapefruit.

"Don't you just love being among all these dead people?" I asked, gesturing to the surroundings.

"Well, to be honest, I actually think that part is a little weird. I would like nothing better than to leave this cemetery, make sure you get home safely, and then curl up in my bed with a tall glass of diluted ginger ale."

How sweet of him, to say something that didn't make sense for a vampire to say. I casually thrust my neck towards him, bathing it in the moonlight.

"Is your neck OK?" he asked.

"I don't know. Is it? What do you think, Edwart?" I massaged it suggestively, suggesting that I had slept on a pile of coals.

"Does it hurt?" he asked.

I had to think fast. Did he want for it to hurt? Was that some kind of weird vampire thing where they prefer to bite necks that hurt, the way my mother had always told me that the way you know a piece of fruit is ripe is that it looks like it hurts?

"Um, y-yes," I stammered, silently thanking the forces that be for the improv class I took last summer. "It hurts. It hurts terribly."

Then something magical happened. Edwart poked my neck. Fire rushed through my entire body. I grabbed his finger, intoxicated by its caress, and gasped for air like a fish out of water gasps for less air. He patted my neck a few times. I wondered if he was putting alcohol on it, the way doctors do before giving you shots.

"How does that feel?" he asked.

"Like, happy." The truth was, it felt completely indescribable. A patch of blackberries—that's how I would describe it.

"Okay, great!" he said, and stopped." That was quick!"

"Oh, um, you know what?" I said, improvising again. "It hurts again. Worse. Much, much worse. Say! I have an idea! You could *bite me*, and then *I would never feel pain again*."

He gave me a look like I was crazy–crazy in love—just as the ground began to shake violently.

"What's happening? Is this part of the transformation process?" I asked, a little unnerved.

"An earthquake?" Edwart suggested with the coldly calculating reasoning of a vampire.

Suddenly the ground split open beneath us, cracking the tombstone in half, and from the grave emerged a figure with bloodstained fangs and a black cape whose tall, curved collar was neatly pressed down in obvious defiance of the current trends.

"Are y-y-you . . . the Leather King?" I managed to ask.

"No," said the figure. "You seriously don't recognize me?"

I looked at him closely: the pale face, the cape, the red eyes, the ridiculously large fangs. I couldn't place him.

"Um, do I know you from work?" I strained to remember if he was one of my co-workers. I strained to remember if I had a job.

"Goodness gravy, Belle—I sit next to you everyday in English!"

"I'm sorry—every face at school kind of blends into one conglomerate dull face except for the face of Edwart Mullen, the love of my life."

He clapped his hands slowly, sinisterly. "Well congratulations to *you two*," he said. "I hope you have a *really* happy life forever and ever in your sweet little house behind a neatly mowed lawn. What you two have is special—you know that? *Really* special. We're all *very* jealous of your overwhelming love for one another."

"Thank you."

"To get on with my point, I'm Joshua. A Vampire. I don't mean to be rude, but you two are trespassing on my grave property right now. I'm truly sorry about all this Belle—honestly I think you're very attractive, even though you don't wear makeup or pay attention to the fashions. To make a confession, I had every intention of asking you to prom the first week of school. But now I'm going to have to take your lives, unfortunately, to nourish myself."

I balked. Another vampire? I guess it made sense; the states of the Pacific Northwest were known for their lenient monster laws.

Next to me, Edwart screamed and covered his eyes, likely visualizing his triumph over this flamboyantly cos- tumed vampire. I relaxed, comfortably settling into the gravestone, ready to watch what every girl hopes to experi- ence once: a real-life vampire fight.

"Not so fast, Josh," I said from my seat. "Cut him up into little bits and burn them, Edwart!"

"*What*? Why would I do that? Why would I ever *ever* do that?" he pondered and then gave me a sharp look. "No! I am not pondering that, Belle! I am hysterically yelling right now. I am experiencing the greatest fear I have ever felt in my life."

Edwart was visibly shaking—I think that happens when vegetarian vampires haven't eaten a bear in a while or something.

"Edwart, we don't have time to have another DTR talk right now. There's *another* vampire now, and I don't think he's familiar with Peter Singer's *The Ethics of What We Eat*."

"*Another* vampire?" he looked behind his shoulder. "Where's the first?" he quavered, most likely from hunger. He gave me another sharp look. "NO! Stop that! I am not quavering from hunger! That doesn't even make sense."

"Come on, Edwart," I cajoled. "He's a vampire, you're a vampire: get to work!"

"Stop, Belle! This is serious—this is not a good time to role-play."

"Role-play?"

"Yeah, role-play. Like that time we role-played that I could lift Tom Newt's car, or when we role-played that I could reach speeds of up to a hundred mph. Or the one where I had to wear vampire teeth and tell you how much I wanted to drain out all your blood when I first laid eyes on you." He froze. "Whoa. Some of this stuff is starting to come together."

I turned to Joshua, signaling that we needed some time to work this out.

"You know what?" Joshua said. "Even though I am a real vampire, which means by nature I am aloof and hot-tempered, I will give you guys some time. Don't mind me— I'll stand right here, silently seething and flashing my eyes."

"So all this time you thought I was a *vampire?*" Edwart whispered furiously, pulling me a few inches to the left.

"Sure," I said, "you know, the lion falls for the lamb . . ."

"What?"

"Sorry. It's easier for me if I explain things in animal terms."

"So you thought I was a . . . lamb?"

"No, a lion. Or, you know, you're the shark and I'm the seal."

He stared at me blankly.

"Okay," I tried again. "You're the giraffe and I'm the leaf."

"Are you breaking up with me?" he asked quietly.

"Of course not," I said tenderly. "Only if you're not a vampire."

"But I'm not a vampire."

"But . . . you are kind of a control freak. In a vampire way."

"You *made* me boss you around! And while we're being honest, you're my first girlfriend, and before I met you I was doubtful that I had the requisite mouth muscles to speak aloud."

I felt my entire monster-hierarchy, with Edwart Vampires at the top, realigning dramatically. "But what about the time that we were talking about different kinds of blood and you kept talking about how each one has its own unique merits, just like different types of wine you said, and then you went on like a fifteen-minute rant about blood homogenization, and then you went into that elaborate mnemonic about the various steps to take while drinking blood? You know, the five S's: suck, sip, swirl . . . swirl again . . . and then . . ."

"Simmer."

"Yeah, simmer."

"Wasn't there another one?"

"I think so—I have it written down on some little cards at home."

"So then how are you not a vampire?" I asked, purpose-fully not inflecting my voice at the end of my question for a lawyer effect.

"Belle, I'm . . . I'm sorry. I'm not a vampire. I'm only a *moderate* blood drinker. I like my hamburgers *medium*-rare."

"Okay, we all set?" asked Josh, tossing another shriv-eled mole onto a pile. *How civilized*, I thought, to have a designated place for appetizer-refuse, just like a good host providing a bowl to put shrimp tails in.

"I guess so," I said. "Get him, Edwart!"

"No Belle— I can't fight a monster! I will never live up to your abnormal and perverse fantasies!"

That hurt. Plenty of teenage girls wished their boyfriends were vampires. Durkheim would blame the val-ues of society for this. I pretty much agreed the problem came from some other place external to my brain.

"I'm getting the hell out of here!" Edwart said, begin-ning to back away. "If you love me, let's go!"

"But Edwart!" I called after him. "We have to defeat this vampire! Are you just going to leave me alone here with him?"

"Isn't that what you want?"

Well that proved it. A real vampire would have been sucking my blood as he said this. I watched as Edwart disap-peared into the fog, this time not in a magical way but in a loud, falling way, signifying that he had tripped over a gravestone. Josh and I watched as he reappeared, hurdling over the gravestones as he jogged. Each time he fell, he screamed, looked back over his shoulder at us, and clambered up to his pigeon-toed feet.

Josh and I sat there, an awkward silence quickly setting in. I took out my little Edwart-keepsake knapsack. I hated to do this in front of a stranger, but I needed some release. Determinedly, I began to burn the items one-by-one: my biology lab report, my stuffed Dracula, some firewood I chopped during our hiking trip, the chunk of hair I pulled from that waitress at Buca di Beppo. I felt better after that.

"Hmm," I said cheerfully, "should we tell ghost stories?"

"I'm not sure you're aware of the peril of your situation, Belle. You see—I am a hungry, amoral vampire, and you are a vulnerable, blood-filled mortal girl. Nonetheless, I would like to share with you one ghost story. I call this story, 'The Tale of the Long Ago Locket,'" Josh said in a shaky ghost voice.

I had definitely heard that story before. I hummed to keep myself from falling asleep.

"What's the matter?" asked Josh. "Aren't you interested? It's a *really* scary story."

"I know it is. I saw it on an episode of *Are You Afraid of the Dark?*"

Josh glowered at me. "Most sad," he said. "It's too bad you know so much about ghost stories. Tell me, do you know what a mortal girl's best means of survival is when a vampire advances?" he asked, advancing.

I yawned. "Yeah, I think I've seen that episode too."

He leaned in close. "Run. The answer is, *run*," he said, crouching down into pre-pounce position.

Suddenly, I panicked, rolling out of post-pounce position. This was wrong, all wrong! I was supposed to be bitten by Edwart and become a vampire myself! I wasn't supposed to be bitten by some strange vampire and die! Everyone knows there is a fine, finicky line between eternal-life-as-vampire v. death-as-a-human.

"I hope you like dying." Josh spoke calmly and confidently, like the way you might speak to your mashed potatoes.

As he took another step towards me, out of the corner of my eye I saw Edwart, bruised and battered after finally surpassing all those gravestones, fleeing out of the gate as Joshua leaned in to bite.

9. INVITATION

PARALYZED WITH FEAR, I STRUGGLED TO REMEMBER
the rules of fighting I learned from Cardio Kicks: 1) You go
girl! 2) Work it! 3) C'mon, ladies, ten more reps!

None of those rules would work. Josh's teeth were four
inches from my throat and it was only a matter of time before
he halved it, and then his teeth would only be two inches
away. Then one inch. Then one-half . . . one-quarter . . . one-
eighth . . . one-sixteenth . . . Suddenly, I remembered Zeno's
paradox. *As long as Josh kept moving towards my throat in half
integrals, he could never reach it.*

However, he did not move towards me in half
integrals—he moved towards me in a single lunge. Abandon-
ing logic, I settled for my krav maga training, picking up the
bench to my left and throwing it at him. It crumbled upon
impact. *Of course.* All the traditional glass benches in Oregon

had recently been replaced with safety glass benches. Thinking fast, I squatted and jumped high to intimidate Josh with my combat training. But Josh didn't retreat. Instead, he assumed Warrior One pose. That was my idea! My only idea.

Well, I thought, *I could always use those nunchucks I carry with me.* I pulled them from my socks and began to swing them above my head. I wondered if they could twirl so much that I would be lifted from the earth, but before I could contemplate where I'd fly, Josh struck me first, hard, in the stomach.

I flew backwards into a gravestone. *Thank God I'm not in a ballet studio full of mirrors!* I thought with relief. Then I heard the sweetest sound I could imagine: a deep, guttural "meow." That's when I knew I was dead. That sound—the only one I wanted to hear—was calling me to the only heaven I wanted to go to: Cat Heaven.

I opened my eyes to see a black cat rubbing gently against my legs. Never mind, I was alive. No wonder I thought it was an angel; the way it purred reminded me of the way Edwart mumbled.

That's when I decided to *really* fight. I jumped up to kick Josh in the butt. I got kind of embarrassed mid-kick, though, so it ended up being more of a timid toe-tap. His butt cheeks jiggled, unscathed, sending me backwards into the empty grave he had come out of.

I was staring at the night sky, dazed, when Josh's head blocked my view of the moon. He swiftly moved forwards, as if to attack, but then stopped. Had my toe-tap sent him the wrong signal? He stood up straight at the edge of the grave, looking down at me. For the first time I noticed how tall he was. Actually, from where I was sitting, he seemed really, really tall. I like tall guys. The two things I look for in a guy is how tall he is and whether or not he's a vampire. Pretty much all my crushes have been one or the other. One guy, actually, was both big and a vampire, but he turned out to be gay.

"Die!" he growled.

"Help!" I screamed.

"Shhh!" everyone at the burial next to us whispered.

"Sorry," we said together. He pulled me out of the grave and we continued struggling in silence.

We fought for a while, occasionally forgetting which of us was the human and which was the vampire. At one point, he was wearing my dress and I was wearing his cape. I was about to bite, but then, for a second, I thought I saw something redeemable beneath those red eyes and that cape and that face made pale by white powder.

"Are you the boy who reads *Romeo and Juliet* every day at lunch?" I asked suddenly.

"*No,* Belle. Jeez Louise! I sit at the table behind you and your friends, with all my brothers and sisters."

I thought back to the tables in the cafeteria: Edwart's table, Jocks, Populars (my table), Arty Kids, Vampires. He must have sat at the last one.

Seeing me sit down and open a yearbook to finally sort this out, Josh continued: "Remember that first day in the cafeteria when we both reached for the cottage cheese at the same time? And then we both tried to pass it off like we were actually reaching for the fries but really we were just waiting for the other person to leave so we could get the cottage cheese? Or the second day when I saved you from getting hit by a car in the school parking lot?"

He spoke like someone from a far, far away time, like middle school. It was so charming! His sentences were so long, I realized, I could easily run away. I could actually have run away at any point, but something kept me there, even when Josh turned away to yell into the darkness.

"Vicky!" he called. "How is the video going?"

"Got it all on tape!" a small female vampire said, running out from behind a tombstone. She was holding a camcorder. I could tell she was evil because she had wavy red hair, a weird smile, and she was wearing a shaggy fur poncho thing.

"I thought this would make a dramatic place for our home movie," Josh gestured to the graveyard. "How would you like to be a movie star?" he asked me menacingly.

Before I could answer, Vicky rushed over to fix my hair and apply glue-in fangs in my mouth.

"What movie?" I asked incredulously. I hadn't signed any release. My fight moves were copyrighted.

"It's called 'A Day in the Life of Josh and Vicky!'" Vicky said. "We started filming this morning when we woke up, and we continued throughout the day. It's been really fun, especially when I filmed Josh doing his homework."

I made a home movie once, right before I left Phoenix forever. I dressed up and danced in the ballet outfit I used to wear when I was a toddler. My mom loved it.

"I have an idea," Vicky continued. "Belle, why don't you say something on tape? How about 'Great to meet you, Josh and Vicky! Thanks for not eating me!'"

Vicky held up the camera. I looked from vampire to vampire. I gulped, swallowing a bug. It felt like my knees were missing.

"Memories are so important, don't you think?" Vicky said.

I said my line quickly to cover up my mispronunciation of the difficult foreign word "to." I know it's either pronounced like "two" or "too" but I always forget which one.

"Now kiss!" Vicky whispered. The camera was still rolling.

Josh closed his eyes and puckered his lips. He leaned forwards. Only a few minutes ago, he wanted to kill me, which I guess was fair, because I wanted to gouge him in the armpit. Still, some of his sharp teeth were popping out of his puckered lips, and I was wary. What if my acting was bad?

Then I remembered that I am a great actress. I closed my eyes and leaned in. We kissed. I didn't feel anything, though, because it was all part of a day's work by that point. It occurred to me that kissing was the least productive part of human courtship and not very sanitary, either. That's how desensitized acting had made me.

"Okay, great!" Vicky said, shutting off the camera. "I'll see you tomorrow morning for "The Next Day in the Life of Josh and Vicky!" she shouted, disappearing into a nearby grave.

Yes, I decided. *She's evil.*

My lips were bleeding a little, so I hastily wiped them off. What would I tell my dad? I decided I would tell him I picked at them to make them red, just like I used to before I was old enough to wear lipstick. Josh was looking at me with hungry eyes.

"Man, it rains a lot here!" I said to fill the silence. "Like *so much.* So . . . ah . . . should we keep fighting or what?"

Josh lunged forwards and pressed his lips to mine again. I resisted a little bit at first, to make it seem like I was that kind of girl—the kind of girl who doesn't like vampires—but then he "French-kissed" me. *So weird!* I had heard about this before, but nothing could have prepared me for such a strange feeling. Even after he removed his nose from my armpit, I still felt a slight tingling sensation.

"So is it awkward if I ask what our status is?" I asked quickly. Not that I cared either way. I just wanted to *know*, you know?

"Not at all. We're a couple now."

Hmm. I wondered how I'd express that on Facebook. I'd have to change it from what it was before: "It's complicated with a vampire." But then I realized that worked pretty well with the new scenario.

"Want to come to the vampire prom with me tonight?" Josh asked.

I remembered my last prom: the stupid pre-prom photos, the ugly pink dresses, the tacky disco ball, the gunshots, the 911 calls, the national media coverage, and the lame cover band.

"Of course!" I said.

"Great, because I already got you a ticket."

"Oh wait," I said, suddenly remembering the boy who had flailed away just minutes ago. "I think I might already be going with someone . . ."

"Another vampire?"

"No. I thought so, but no."

Remembering Edward I felt angry, and a little silly. I should have known he wasn't a vampire. He failed to meet the three telltale criteria for vampirism: speaking in an old-timey way, being pompous, and having sparkly skin.

"Well, it doesn't really matter," Josh said. "We vampires have a separate school prom in winter instead of spring. Coincidentally at a time most inconvenient for outdoor photos." He sneered. "Separate but equal my ass."

I shook my head in sympathy. I had never realized that being a vampire made you different, but not in a nice Dr. Seuss kind of way in which you have a star on your belly.

We sat down to snuggle in front of a tomb.

"Josh," I asked. "How did you become a vampire?"

"I fought Dracula. I nearly killed him, too, only I felt bad when he told me that I was his only friend, and that was the reason he'd kept me in his dungeon for five years. He bit me right when I turned to go back to my dungeon. What a trickster! Very loyal once you've known him for a few centuries, though."

"You know Dracula?!" I yelled. "That's so cool!"

I imagined what I'd do if I ever met Dracula. I'd probably say, "I'm Belle Goose, girl of the vampires," and he would bow down and nip my feet.

"Well, Belle," Josh said. "I'm a pretty cool guy."

"What was Dracula like?"

"Fang-ed. Bat-like."

Wow. Dating Josh would lead me to all sorts of opportunities. Maybe he knew the Swamp Thing too.

"I'll take you to your house before we go to the prom," Josh said, standing up and brushing off his cape. "You'll probably want to put some makeup on or something. Wash your face a few times."

I blushed. I hadn't realized my tempting blood smell was coming from my nose pores.

We held hands as we walked towards the exit. Josh's hand was cold, but not in the clammy sweaty way I was used to. *Edwart*, I thought with a sigh. *Edwart, Edwart.* Where did I know that name from?

"Wait here, beautiful," Josh said once we exited the cemetery gate. "I'm going to bring the car around."

A few minutes later he came to a rolling stop by the curb. "Get in," he said ferociously.

Okay. I thought. *That was a little rude.* But I didn't say anything, not then, and not even when he hopped out, blindfolded me and tied my arms together.

"It's for your own good, clumsy,"

It was hard for me to argue with that, especially as I was falling into the car.

He buckled my seatbelt. A few minutes later, I was surprised to feel the car move so slowly and responsibly under Josh's control. But, then again, he had been driving since the invention of cars.

We stopped. "Here's the plan: you're going to go upstairs and clean yourself up and get rid of that human smell," Josh said. I was still blindfolded, but I assumed we were at my house, or some other place that had an upstairs. "I am going to smooth-talk your Dad."

He took off my blindfold. I stumbled towards my door, but he stopped me mid-step and put down his cape for me to walk on so my shoes wouldn't get dirty from the pavement. I thanked him, gingerly stepping on the red satin lining. He quickly lifted up the corners, bagging me, and carried me to the door.

"What would you do without me, Belle?" he asked, inserting a tracking device in my ear.

His behavior was unusual, but I had never dated a vampire before. Besides, who could blame Josh for being possessive? I was special—a girl who would one day be on a talk show saying: "Yes, Diane, my childhood *was* difficult."

Shrugging, I reached in my purse for my key, which turned out to not be necessary. Josh melted a hole in the door and tossed me through it.

"Move, move, move!" he yelled. "We've got a vampire prom to get to!"

10. VAMPIRE PROM

I RAN UPSTAIRS AS QUICKLY AS POSSIBLE, THEN TORE off my shirt and threw it on the floor.

"Might I suggest you wear something simple?" a voice directed without any hint of suggestion.

I turned to the window and gasped. *Josh*! Quickly, I covered up my bra-patterned undershirt. It was too late, though; Josh had seen them. *So now he knew I was aware of lady garments.*

"I don't mean to control every facet of your life," he continued, taking my hand and closing the window with it, "but I believe it would be unwise for you to wear something eye-grabbing to the prom. The theme is Fancy Venetian Masquerade, and you're going to be in a room full of vampires. Any fabric you own that camouflages with walls or dance floors might be best."

"How did you get in here?"

"Through the window—*duh* I'm a vampire!"

"Still, my window is barely two feet tall."

"*Duh,* I did the vampire trick where you shrink your-self down with a vampire ray and then vampire-pump your-self back to a normal size."

I started to ask more questions, but we were inter-rupted by a violent banging on the door.

"Where is he?" called Jim. "Is that vampire in there?"

Josh lunged towards me and put his hand over my mouth. "*Noooo,*" he said in a low, masculine voice. "*Just your female, human daughter . . . all alone.*"

I pushed his hand away. "No, Dad," I said. "I don't see a vampire in here. We'll keep looking though! I mean, *I'll* keep looking though!"

After a long pause, we heard him stomp back down the stairs.

I turned to Josh. "I can't believe you told him you were a vampire! Jim *hates* vampires."

"Are you embarrassed by me?" he asked teasingly. He grabbed my waist and pulled me close. "What about now?" he said, doing a humiliating penguin dance.

"No—I'm not embarrassed by you. We just have to keep your vampirism a secret from my friends and family forever and ever, okay?"

He stopped dancing. "Whoa there. Forever and ever?"

I sighed exasperatedly. Edwart might have been clueless

but he didn't ask *half* as many questions. "*Yes*, forever and ever. Once you've bitten me and made me your vampire mate."

He slowly backed away. "Wait right here, Belle," he said, opening the window behind his back. "There's something I got to do . . . at this other place."

As I heard his car roar to life and then screech away, I turned my attention to my closet. *What could I possibly wear to a masquerade?* I threw everything I owned onto my bed. Leg cast, left leg cast, neck cast, various finger casts. In the end, I decided to go with my full-body cast.

A car screeched to a halt outside our house. I heard voices floating up from the living room. Josh had returned! I crept to the doorway, listening for the sounds of Jim breaking his rifle out of its mounted glass case. He must have convinced Jim that he wasn't a vampire, though, because all I heard was the low hum of their conversation.

"I assure you I'm a very old-fashioned guy, Mr. Goose. I promise to do everything by the book," Josh was saying. "Here is the agreement that the learned man in the next town over drew up for me. It says that in exchange for one date with your daughter, I will provide you with four laying geese, a bundle of barrel staves, and the use of my largest scythe in three weeks' time."

"This pleases me," said Jim. "I am an extremely permissive father who would never dream of requesting such an arrangement, but I am professedly a sucker for barrel staves. Share a celebratory pint with me?"

I heard the *glug-glug* sound of gin being poured into pint glasses.

"Only two for me, Mr. Goose," said Josh. "I'm driving."

"What was it you said you were again, Josh my boy?"

I inhaled sharply and shut my eyes tight. *Don't say vampire.*

"A graffiti artist, sir. A window graffiti artist."

"I see."

Suddenly, the sound of glass shattering rang throughout the house. Josh sprang up the stairs into my room, slamming the door shut behind him. Jim barreled up the stairs after him, getting more and more aggravated the more he shot his rifle, sinking the priceless, antique bullets into our seventeenth-century Frisian wainscoting.

"What did I say?" Josh gasped, moving my dresser in front of the door.

"Jim's a window-wiper, Josh. And according to a T-shirt he has, he is also a Female Body Inspector. I think that's some type of gynecologist, but I've always been too grossed out to ask. In any case," I explained, "he *hates* window graffiti artists. Really, the only people he doesn't hate are descendents of werewolves. Try that next time."

"What are you *wearing?*" asked Josh, admiring my costume.

"You like it? It's a full-body cast."

"What are you supposed to be? Some kind of creepy mummy?"

"Yes," I said uncomfortably. I was a little hurt that he

couldn't tell I was a beautiful cocoon. Maybe we weren't meant to raise three Dachshunds together, after all. "What are *you* supposed to be?" I asked.

Josh was wearing a formal black tuxedo with a smoky, grey vest. "I'm a Human Guy," he said with a grin, flashing his false human teeth.

I shuddered. *Why do boys insist on wearing the most unattractive outfits they can find to costume parties?* I wondered just as Jim shot down the door.

"You!" he said, pointing his rifle at Josh. He fired.

BANG!

Josh zoomed left, supernaturally avoiding the bullet.

BANG!

Josh leaped right, humanly avoiding the bullet.

My dad reloaded. First, he poured in the gunpowder. Then, he pushed it down with a long brush-like thing and added the musket ball. Right then, I bet Jim really regretted buying that Revolutionary War rifle, even though he got it for an incredible price. It took about ninety seconds to re-load. It doesn't sound like that long, but try waiting in silence for even five seconds. It feels very long.

One . . .

Two . . .

Three . . .

Four . . .

Five . . .

See what I'm talking about?

"Relax, Dad," I said, before this ridiculous waste of paper could go any further. "He's a werewolf."

Jim lowered his rifle. "Oh. Sorry about that," he mumbled. He looked over at my costume. "Wow, Belle. You look like a real mature lady!"

I had to admit, I *did* look stunning for a caterpillar's pupal casing. Lucy and Laura would say I looked more "hAwWt and jUiCaYyY ;)" but I think that "stunning" was a much better word. I had recently come into the possession of a Thesaurus. You would not believe how many words there are! When I opened that book, I was like, whoa! Word party!

After we had picked the bullets out of the wall, we went downstairs to perform the traditional father-meets-date ritual.

"So . . . Josh. How's school?" inquired Jim.

"Good."

"Hmmm. Uh are you into sports at all?"

"No. Do you mind if I take my false teeth out? It's hard to speak with them in." He popped them out and bared his sharp, pointy fangs. I could see Jim's blood rushing in terror to Jim's right leg—the farthest place from Josh's teeth it could go.

"Have you, uh, seen any movies lately?"

"Why would you ask that?" Josh said, calmly wrapping a tourniquet around Jim's leg. It was now bulging with blood. Delicious, nutritious blood.

"Well, you know . . . it's just one of those questions you ask werewolves. Every werewolf likes movies, right?" My dad chuckled knowingly.

"That's a pretty bold generalization to make, Mr. G. Can you hold still for a second?" Josh pulled a syringe from his pocket and began to extract blood from Jim's leg.

"I'm not being prejudiced! Believe me, some of my best friends are werewolves."

"Well, frankly, *I'm* more of a television guy. Have you ever seen *True Blood*? It's about vampires. It's entertaining, but not very realistic. I mean, a synthetic blood that satisfies vampires? Come on! You need the real thing. Preferably from a teenage girl. All right, Belle—you ready?"

"Yep!" I stood up, showing off the smooth pleats in my cast. I began to spin around gracefully, but once I started it was hard to stop. I felt like a figure skater—both in my grace and my desire to throw up.

Josh finally grabbed my shoulders to stop me. "Stop, Belle. That will do."

I smiled back at him and looked deep into his giant soulless vampire pupils. He glanced coldly into mine.

"Now I know why they call you Belle," he said softly. "Did you know Belle means beautiful in Spanish?"

"I'm pretty sure you're thinking of Fr—"

"Shhhh," said Josh, effectively shushing me, "Let Josh do the talking from now on."

He was so charming.

"I'll have your stupid daughter back by midnight,

Mr. G," he said. "You can have this back." He threw the syringe of blood back at him, "I think I'm all set."

"You wanna come over for the Seahawks game on Sunday?" Jim asked. Jim was lonely. He really didn't have a lot of friends besides that wheelchair guy.

"I'm all set, Mr. G. Football games are usually during the day, and you know . . ." he said, sheepishly gesturing towards his skin and making sparkle motions with his hands.

"I don't understand. My other werewolf friend watches football all the time."

"Okay, bye Dad!" I called.

Josh steered me out the door towards his black limousine. Before he shoved me in, he looked me up and down. "Hey Belle, do you know what your volume is?"

"What?" I replied, trying to think if a sphere or a cylinder were a better representation of my body type.

"Like how much blood you have in your body."

"I . . . I don't know. First I'd have to figure out what my radius is, Josh." I had decided that cylinder worked best because of the flat surface of my skull.

On our way to the prom, Josh insisted on giving me a driving lesson. He propped his feet up on the dashboard and shouted "Gas!" or "Break!" at me as I manned the pedals below the driver's seat. He was such a controlling driver—not once did he let me improvise. I couldn't even control the radio from where I sat cramped on the ground. Josh blared his techno vampire songs. None of them were Schubert.

Since the theme was a Fancy Venetian Masquerade, you would think the prom would be better decorated—there were a couple of black streamers and one overly inflated black balloon. But then I told myself to be more open-minded. Most craft and party stores close before sundown. If a vampire went in daylight, he would look like he was stealing a lot of glitter by rubbing it all over his body. What a mess that would be, legally.

"I hope you don't find the costumes boring," Josh said apologetically, as we walked through the gymnasium to get to the photographer. "The prom committee picked a pretty unimaginative theme in terms of costumes this year. Looks like everyone decided to be human—there's a huge human-romance-novel phenomenon going on in the vampire world right now. You should have seen the costumes for the last few prom themes: Pimps and their Street Ho's; CEOs and their Office Ho's; GI Joes and their Combat Ho's; Gardeners and their Garden Hoes; Firemen and their Fire Hose . . . If you ask me, a 'masquerade' theme isn't flattering for anyone's features, nor does it define the appropriate gender roles very clearly."

"It's brilliant," I said, but a little part of me wished I had Edwart by my side instead of this breathtakingly beautiful vampire. Someone who would always be there to look more awkward than me.

Josh and I paused to take a prom photo. It came out beautifully, even though it looked like my date was just a bunch of clothes hanging in the air. Still, the light caught the silken fibers of his suspended tie magnificently.

As we walked towards the punch bowl, I couldn't help but think that Josh was ashamed to have me as his date. Maybe it was the way he kept mouthing "She's not with me," at passersby. I don't know. I have trouble understanding boys' signals sometimes. As the saying goes, boys are from Mars and girls are from a completely normal planet.

When all of the vampires broke into a choreographed dance, I sank deeper into a feeling of alienation. When did they all find time to practice together? The zombie-style dance was actually pretty good, but I think many of the moves were heavily influenced by a certain video by a certain immortalized King of Pop— "Black or White."

I stood by the punch table as the vampires danced through the last verse. There were four bowls labeled, "AB positive," "O negative," "AB negative," and "Grab Bag."

"I'll have an AB positive," I told Josh when he returned from the dance floor. "What's it made of? Apples and Bananas?"

"It's made of blood, Belle. You know this is blood, right?"

"Oh, of course. I was just joking," I replied, sipping from my cup in horror. I was really going to have to commit to this.

As I nursed my blood cup, Josh introduced me to his friends, Levi and Zeke. They gawked at my costume.

"What are you staring at?" I asked defensively. "At least *I* have a costume."

"Whoa!" said Levi. "Say that again!"

"Say what again?"

"Ha! Did you hear that Zeke? She sounds *sooo* human."

"Hello," said Zeke in a deep, even voice. "My name is Human Guy."

A group of vampires gathered around us, laughing.

"Oooh, let me try let me try!" said one. "Hello. My name is Human Guy."

They all laughed again.

"Hello," said Levi. "I am a Human person."

"Why do humans say it like that?" Zeke said. "Humans always say it like that!"

"Nobody says that!" I told them, but this only made them laugh harder.

"Hello," said Josh. "My name is Mr. Human Guy." They were weeping with laughter.

"*Josh*," I whispered ferociously. "Aren't you going to *defend* me?"

"Come on, Belle—you know how you sound. It's not your fault," he added quickly. "It's an inherent flaw within your species. I know you can't help it and will never be able to correct it." He held my cast-covered chin in his hand and petted my cast-covered hair. "Be proud of who you are, Belle. Don't apologize for your differences. Your quirky, defective differences."

Just then, someone tapped me on the shoulder.

"Belle!" cried a familiar voice. I spun around to see none other than Lucy!

"Lucy, what are you doing here?"

She laughed maniacally. "Belle, I bought over a dozen

prom dresses because you couldn't tell me which one was best. I mean, these dresses aren't just going to wear themselves! This is my fifth prom this week."

"But— you don't even like vampires! I like vampires. This is *my* thing. Who even invited you?"

"Levi invited me." She lowered her voice and spoke directly in my ear. "Belle Goose if you ruin my chance at being prom queen tonight I will make sure that you live long enough to witness the passing of your loved ones." She smiled and trotted away to join Levi on the dance floor.

"Come on, Belle," said Josh. "This is my favorite song—let's dance!"

"I really don't want to dance."

"*Dance with me*, Belle," he growled.

"Seriously Josh? To Green Day? They've been around *forever*."

"Wrong," he barked. "They've only been around for the past twenty proms."

"What? Twenty proms!"

"Yeah, this is my eighty-sixth prom. I'm immortal, remember?"

"Yeah, I know that, I guess I just never . . . really . . . thought this out." Again, I pined for Edwart. Edwart, who would never let it slip that he'd been to eighty-six proms because he had no idea who Green Day was.

"Dance," Josh commanded.

"You don't know what you're asking for," I warned.

"Just *once*," he ordered.

"Seriously, Josh—I've never danced without unwittingly causing a political uprising."

"*One dance*," he decreed, pulling me onto the dance floor and manipulating me like a puppet using the pulleys that were still attached to my full-body cast.

"Okay okay—I'll do *one* dance." I did my ironic tap-dance. It's a complicated routine, but onlookers will mistake your clumsiness for irony if you raise your eyebrows enough.

As predicted, when I finished there was a revolution.

A mob of outraged vampires swarmed the dance floor, frantically trying to stop the tap-dancing that had now gotten out of control. One hundred tap-dancing vampires were shoving and kicking each other in attempts to complete the routine. I slipped away to the wall unharmed as a couple tap-dancers, aggravated by the oppressive handling of the mob, violently overhauled the speakers, cutting the music. The gym filled with the din of the crowd's antics. One vampire dove onto the punch table like it was a Slip'n Slide while his friends poured the contents of the bowls onto themselves and splashed around. Another vampire, offended by the splashing, tossed his blood punch into a splasher's eyes and threw a superfluous punch. This polarized the vampires into two teams: pro-splashers and anti-splashers.

I waited patiently for the riot to subside, sipping my blood punch in a folding chair in the corner, too bored to even say I told you so (but not too bored to broadcast it over the PA system).

I saw Lucy being pummeled as she tried to escape the surging masses.

"Watch out!" I shouted, but it was too late. Someone had grabbed her by the dress, loosening a carefully fixed safety pin on her sleeve.

"Ouch!" she said, examining the prick on her arm. A drop of blood oozed out.

The vampires stopped rioting. They all got really quiet and started to lick their lips, closing in on Lucy. I started to lick my lips, too, because it's one of those subconscious, contagious things like sneezing, but then I stopped because it just isn't worth it if you forgot to bring ChapStick.

The drop trickled down her arm and onto the floor. Three vampires lunged for it at once. Another drop trickled down. Three more vampires dove to the floor. That's when her hemophilia kicked in. The blood started spurting from her arm like water from a fire hydrant. The vampires held their faces up and opened their mouths to catch the blood, some twirling around and playing in the crimson torrents like kids on a hot summer day.

"Prick her!" Lucy cried, pointing at me. "She's human too! Prick her!"

A few vampires glanced my way. I smiled and waved at them generously. I was their Il Duce, the face of the revolution.

"Get her!" The vampires cried. Suddenly, I was the most popular girl at the prom. The crowd mobilized over to my chair and hoisted me up on their shoulders. They started chanting enthusiastically, saying, "Go humans! More human blood! Bring her to the stage! More human blood! Prick her arm! More human blood!"

Despite my newfound popularity, I was still quite surprised when they announced over the loudspeaker, "And tonight's Prom King and Queen are . . . Joshua Vampyre and Belle Goose!"

Four vampires set me down on the stage next to Josh before settling back into the audience with a crazed, hungry glint in their eyes.

"I can't believe I'm Prom Queen!" I whispered excitedly to Josh.

"I know," he said, wrapping his arm around me. "I can't believe you're Prom Queen either. To me, you'll always be my Prom Minion."

I frowned. Suddenly, nothing seemed right. Lucy, trying to escape from a dozen hungry vampires; Josh's domineering yet somehow not romantic attitude towards me; our being crowned prom King and Queen when it obviously should have been given to a different couple—one that had shown more courage—the gay vampire dancing with his boyfriend in the corner. Despite the disapproving glances, they weren't going to let anyone else define their love.

The entire gymnasium was cheering us on. Lucy was pointing at the air above my head, screaming something. I looked up where she was pointing to gaze at my tiara. I gasped. Angelica's ominous epileptic message resounded in my brain: *I SEE A ROOM IN CHAPTER TEN. A ROOM*

FULL OF VAMPIRES. IN THE CORNER OF THE ROOM IS A METAL FOLDING CHAIR . . . BEWARE OF THE CROWN.

I ducked in time to narrowly miss the falling fifty-pound dumbbell with a spiky tiara attached. I jumped off the stage.

"Seize her!" Josh cried oppressively.

I turned to face him. "I've had enough of your authoritative commands, Joshua. I'm tired of vampires."

I ran out of the gymnasium into the clear, cool night air, feeling lost and friendless because, let's face it—talking to Jim is like talking to a wall. I had no one to turn to— neither vampire nor human. *God, I need a werewolf friend*, I thought as I walked towards the parking lot.

Then, something funny happened. My vision tunneled, and all I could see was a white, pasty light, glowing on the horizon. I stopped at the top of the stairs leading to the parking lot and steadied myself with the railing. The light continued to glow as pale as ever, but now two green lights were added towards the top, and then a goofy, metal-gridded smile. *Edward*. I was seeing Edward. All of my anxiety and confusion washed away as I realized what I had to do.

First, though, I would need to get down these stairs without hurting myself. With Edward shining like a beacon in my mind, I gazed coolly at the fatal obstacle course lying before me on the steps. I had never felt calmer in my life.

I hopped from one foot to another down the stairs, rolling when necessary as the axes suspended from seemingly out of nowhere dropped all around me. I was doing it! I was really doing it. I swerved around a spike that shot up from the ground. It narrowly missed me, poking a hole in my costume instead. As the clock struck midnight, I could feel my cast cocoon beginning to unravel. *Soon I will turn into a pumpkin.* Or was it a helpless maid? A butterfly? In any case, some objective correlative was changing in a way that implied my character had developed. Most pertinently, in the ability to balance.

But I wasn't done.

Okay, Pretty Face, I said to myself, gaining encouragement from my self-established nickname, *There's one more thing you need to fix before this night is through.*

11. RIGHTFUL PLACE

AND THAT ONE THING WAS ADJUSTING THE ALARM SYSTEM in our house. Now that a vampire breaking into my house and hovering over my bed at night was no longer a deluded fantasy of mine but a frighteningly real possibility, I needed to disable the "Ring for Criminals but Ignore Any Vampires" setting.

I ran back to my house and retrieved the vampire-proof locks from our bottom kitchen drawer. Jim had been on my case about putting those on, but between the vampire fighting and my Elizabeth Bennett-esque romantic realizations, I just hadn't found the time. Remembering that he had warned me I would be sleeping on the streets tonight if he came home and our house still wasn't vampire-proof, I went through all the rooms, applying the safety locks that only human hands can open. This is because human hands can squeeze and pull simultaneously, while vampires and children can only do one or the other at any given time.

I wanted to forget all about prom, so I took off my ragged cast and changed into a slim, satin evening gown. I looked in the mirror, resolved; I looked at a self-portrait I had drawn, resolved; I looked into the dirty water in the kitchen sink, which had a faint reflection, resolved. It was time to go to Edwart.

I arrived over the other side of the fence surrounding his gated neighborhood, panting, realizing I could have walked in the open entrance instead. I decided to take off my heels; they were fine to walk in, but I wanted Edwart to think that I had a hard time getting to him. I also—oops—accidentally ripped my dress climbing over a gate and—oops—accidentally messed up my hair with my hand.

I ran along the streets of Edwart's subdivision in the dark, imagining I was a woman who balances clay pots on her head running to the watering hole, or that I was a gifted teenage girl running away from a group of vampires celebrating the greatest night of high school. A lot had happened to me in the past few days. I had dated a real boy who was a fake vampire. I had dated a real vampire with a fake accent. I had faked my death to see if I would have a big funeral, but I didn't have any funeral at all, because my eye kind of twitched as I was lying there and it ruined everything. I had *finally* gotten through that many-book series about the girl prankster, Nancy Drew. Also there was something about werewolves, but I left that part out.

As I ran, all of these events ran through my mind in a kind of photo-video montage with cool, exhilarating rock music playing in the background. I added the image of me winning some sort of award, because I have a feeling this will happen soon.

I turned down Edwart's street, deciding to walk the rest of the way because I didn't want to be out of breath when I arrived. I wondered what I would say to explain the sweat stains on my dress. Would he believe me if I told him that I had peed? My pee did have a funny way of winding up by my armpits.

I was right in front of Edwart's house when, suddenly, I heard "Decode" by Paramour. My ring tone!

I quickly opened my cell phone. "Wuddup Blood?" I said. Answering this way was a habit I had developed when I thought my boyfriend was a vampire.

"Be careful not to speak until I tell you to."

I froze. *It was Josh!* I dropped the phone. I picked it up and then dropped it again.

I put the phone to my ear just in time to hear him say, "Good, now say 'Switchblade' or press one if that is your current location."

"Switchblade," I whispered, looking up at Edwart's glass house in fear. There could only be one reason behind this call: kidnapping. Would I ever hear Edwart's sweet triangle melody again?

"This is your final warning." Josh continued.

"Stop it!" I yelled. "I'm not afraid of you!"

"Your vehicle is not insured," he said.

"Where's Edwart? Do not hurt him!" Slipping a little, I began to run up the glass walk.

"To insure your car, please press one or say 'INSURE' after the tone." Josh's voice said.

I stopped running, suddenly relaxed. It was a recording. So that's how vampires make a living: using their commanding voices for pre-recorded phone calls.

At Edwart's door, my index finger was too shaky to ring his doorbell—yes, another insecure reservation about our love for one another was preventing me from doing the inevitable. *What if his life were better without me? What if he had found someone within the last four hours who had read* more *Jane Austen novels than me? What if he had found someone who suffered from fewer delusions?* I leaned my head against the wall in self-defeat, accidentally ringing the doorbell.

Edwart opened the door. "Belle!" he cried.

"Edwart!" I cried.

"Belle!"

"Edwart!"

"Belle!"

"Edwart!"

I noticed there was garlic above the doorframe. Edwart held a stake in one hand and a "Team Jacob" shirt in the other.

"Did you get bit?" he asked nervously.

"No," I said, coming towardss him. "I'm fine."

"Phew!" he said. He put down the shirt and stake. "Because *that* would be a twist!"

"Don't worry. If Josh ever tries that I will bite him first and turn him into a girl."

We were silent a few moments. In the first moment, I noted with relief how looking at him still made my heart beat faster. In the second moment, I anxiously wondered if the beating would ever slow down or was I going into cardiac arrest after all that running. In the third moment, I took in his skinny beanpole frame and beaming, freckled face. I couldn't help but beam back. As long as I was with Edwart, I would never lose another thumb war again.

"So what's up?" he said.

I gave the usual answer: "Not much. Just left the vampire prom to come see you."

"Belle, I'm really sorry I left you in the cemetery. I was going to take some karate lessons and then come back for you . . . but after the lesson on ethics I realized that karate begins and ends with courtesy. It is a discipline that should only be used for self-defense, and even *that* as a last resort. So I hiked up Deadman's mountain and got the android—"

"The one that falls and gets up again?"

"Yeah—that one!" He grinned at me, wonderingly. "You remembered."

"Of course Edwart. That was the day that I realized that I could love you even if you devoted all your time to creating a useless, unmarketable android."

"Not exactly useless anymore." He stepped aside, revealing the android behind him. It looked like the same anatomically correct human body imitation as before, but something was off.

"Watch this." Edwart turned it on. Its eyes glowed red.

"Vampire: seven miles away," it said in the voice of Jeff Goldblum ("He was the first robot to ever win an academy award," explained Edwart with admiration). It raised its robotic arm. Attached to it was a huge harpoon-looking weapon.

"It's a cold-seeking missile," said Edwart, smiling mischievously. "I call it a 'vampire shish kabob.'"

"Awesome," I murmured. "Why didn't you use it?"

He looked at his feet. "I heard you were with Josh and . . . I didn't want to hurt him if . . ."

"Why? Why wouldn't you want to protect me from that awful, awful vampire?"

He looked at me with a sad smile and bright, weary eyes. "Would you have liked it if I blew up all the vampires while you were still dating one? Wouldn't you have rather I waited patiently for you to return, no matter how long it took, so we could blow them up together?"

I paused, unsure where this was going.

"So I waited for you," he continued. "I waited to see if you would come back, even though you would rather date a vampire than me."

"Well . . ." I started to say, but then I decided that statement was too complicated to correct. So instead I said: "I'm sorry too, Edwart."

He placed his hand on the android's LAUNCH

button. "Shall we?" he said playfully, holding out his other hand for mine.

"Edwart!"

"What?"

I crossed my arms in disapproval.

"Oh—you thought . . . you thought I was *really* going to . . . you think I would *kill? Kill vampires?*" he laughed uneasily. I laughed too. I had to admit, it would make a pretty good prank some day.

Edwart turned away from me a little but moved his eyes so they were looking at me peripherally.

"Can I . . . show you a video game I made?" he asked quietly.

"Yeah, sure. That's so cool that you make videogames! Is it about me?"

"Well," he said as he turned on his Wii. I realized that my clever deduction was very clever, indeed. Of course it was about me!

"Okay, so this is you," he said pointing to an unflatteringly computer-animated girl.

"But she has brown hair," I said.

"You have brown hair. Don't you?"

"*Brown with red highlights,*" I corrected. Jeez!

He pointed to a muscular warrior character. "This is obviously me," he said, "and this is Josh!" He pointed to a mushroom near the bottom of the screen. "Let's fight him, Belle!"

I was getting a little impatient. Were we going to have

to wait four books and thousands of pages for anything to happen?

"So what do you want to do now?" I asked.

"Play videogames."

"How long do you want to play videogames for?"

"A really long time. I want to play every videogame with you."

"And then after that?"

"Well if there's time we should really work on our club website, but I understand if you get tired after all these videogames. I have two closets full."

I lay back on the couch, exhausted. The problem with smart boys is that they never initiate.

Then, quick as a flash, it happened. In one squeaky scoot across the plastic couch, Edwart was by my side. He swiftly wrapped his arm around me, pulling me towards his bony chest.

His hands grabbed my hands like they were video game controllers. He pushed down on my left index finger. I low-kicked. He pushed down on my left pinkie. I jumped. He pushed down on my right thumb. I paused in mid-air. He kind of rotated my wrist while pushing down on my right middle finger. I crouched down and shot a fireball from my hands. This was getting fun!

Suddenly I blurted out. "I love you more than everything in the entire galaxy combined into one potent, delicious piece of gum!"

"That definitely seems like enough," Edwart said. He

gazed at me in silence for a moment. "This game shows how I feel."

We looked at the Belle and Edwart figures on the TV screen. They were next to each other and bobbing up and down lightly, every so often saying "Hiyah!" *Just like us*, I thought.

Slowly, Edwart began to trace my spine with his fingers, drawing invisible shapes on my back. I turned towards him and traced his hand with my fingers, making an invisible turkey.

After a few minutes, Edwart asked: "What am I drawing?"

"A computer."

He sighed and gently pressed his lips to my hair. "You know me too well," he murmured.

I imagined what the kids at my old school in Phoenix would think if they saw me now. They'd probably think, "Belle left Phoenix? I thought there was someone missing from my history project group!"

We began to butterfly kiss, which is when you touch your eyelashes to the other person's skin. I was going to respect Edwart's desire to wait, and he was going to respect my desire for winged creatures.

"AHHH LEG CRAMP LEG CRAMP!" Edwart suddenly shouted.

"Oh my God, I'm so sorry, did I do something?" I asked, worried that this was getting too intense for him.

"No, I just need to stretch it—okay, that's better."

I lifted up my face towards Edwart's to butterfly kiss him again. He bowed his face towards mine, fluttering his eyelashes softly against my eyelashes, and then against my cheek and lips. Edwart had terrible eyelash-eye coordination, so I held very still to help him out. He firmly cupped my face in his hands for better aim. Then, very slowly, he tilted my face to his. I stopped fluttering my eyelashes. We stared at each other for a very long time. My eyes started going a little cross-eyed and I saw three noses at once. He swept away the hair that was stuck to my ChapStick, weaving his fingers deep into my brownish-red tresses like a finger headband. Tenderly, he drew my lips towards his, and I could feel his breath tickling the tiny hair follicles that every normal woman has above her mouth.

"AHHH FOOT CRAMP FOOT CRAMP!" he yelled.

"How is this happening?"

"It's fine—ow!—it's fine now."

We looked at each other and laughed a little because, hey, relationships take work, and communication.

And with that Edwart put his cold lips to my neck, for the first time.